Case Interview Business Essentials

Your 2-Hour MBA to Ace Consulting Interviews

Taylor Warfield

All rights reserved. No part of this book may be reproduced, distributed, or transmitted in any form by any means, including electronic, mechanical, photocopy, recording, or otherwise, without the prior written permission of the author.

This book and the information contained in this book are for informative purposes only. The information in this book is distributed on an as-is basis, without warranty. The author makes no legal claims and the material is not meant to substitute legal or financial counsel.

The author, publisher, and copyright holder assume no responsibility for the loss or damage caused or allegedly caused, directly or indirectly, by the use of information contained in this book. The author and publisher specifically disclaim any liability incurred from the use or application of the contents of this book.

Throughout this book, trademarked names are referenced. Rather than using a trademark symbol for every occurrence of a trademarked name, we state that we are using the names in an editorial fashion only and to the benefit of the trademark owner, with no intention of infringement of the trademark.

This book contains several fictitious examples that involve names of real people, places, and organizations. Any slights of people, places, or organizations are unintentional.

Copyright © 2025 by Taylor Warfield
All rights reserved

ISBN-13: 978-1-7333381-5-8

Table of Contents

1. Introduction 1
2. Lessons on Profit 7
3. Lessons on Markets 27
4. Lessons on Customers 51
5. Lessons on Companies 67
6. Lessons on Competitive Advantage 89
7. Lessons on Products 101
8. Lessons on Pricing 111
9. Lessons on Operations 123
10. Lessons on Economics 135
11. Lessons on Mergers & Acquisitions 149
12. Lessons on Financial Statements and Terms 161
13. Lessons on Different Industries 179
14. Next Steps 211
15. About the Author 215

1. Introduction

Your 2-Hour MBA

Welcome to your shortcut to consulting interview success.

In the next few hours, you're going to learn everything you need to know about case interview business essentials.

No fluff. No filler. No nonsense.

Just the fastest way to learn all of the essential business concepts, principles, and terminology so that you can nail your case interviews and land that consulting offer.

Whether your interview is months away or even tomorrow, this is your 2-hour MBA crash course on strategy, operations, finance, and industry knowledge that will give you the edge over every other candidate.

I spent $250,000 getting an MBA at the Wharton School of the University of Pennsylvania, one of the top business schools in the world.

I'll help you skip the $250,000 degree and two years of classes by teaching you everything you need to know about business in just a few hours.

Why Business Knowledge Matters

Most candidates spend 90% of their time practicing frameworks, mental math drills, and doing mock cases. However, one thing that many candidates neglect is building a strong business acumen.

While consulting doesn't require you to have a business background or degree, here's the truth.

If you don't understand the fundamentals of business, you'll eventually hit a wall in your case interview preparation:

- You can't solve a market entry case if you're not familiar with the different ways companies can enter new markets

- You can't solve a pricing case if you don't know the different ways to price a product

- You can't give a realistic recommendation if you don't understand the nuances of how different industries work

This book fixes that problem.

In 100 concise, but content-packed lessons, you'll:

- Master core business concepts every consultant uses, from breakeven analysis to pricing strategies to operational improvement

- Know how to answer common case interview business questions, such as the different ways to increase revenue and the most common barriers to entry in a new market

- Familiarize yourself with how 14 different industries work, including drivers of success and key challenges in each

- Understand the language of business and sound like a consultant

By the end of this book, you'll have the business vocabulary, context, and fundamentals to walk into any case interview and sound like you've been doing consulting for years.

Even if you have no business background or experience, you'll be able to understand everything in this book. I'll start with the basics and teach you everything in simple, everyday language.

This isn't about memorizing random facts about businesses.

This is about building a solid foundation of essential business concepts and principles that you can leverage and bring up in your case interviews.

You'll still need to practice actual cases, work on your math, and improve your structuring skills, but with this business knowledge, every one of those other skills will click into place faster.

Who Am I?

Why should you bother learning from me and listening to my advice?

I'm Taylor Warfield, a former Bain Manager, interviewer, and founder of HackingTheCaseInterview.com. I've published a few best-selling books that have sold 50k+ copies worldwide:

- Hacking the Case Interview

- The Ultimate Case Interview Workbook

- Case Interview Math, Math, Math

- Hacking the PM Interview

- How to Write a Resume That Doesn't Suck

My YouTube channel, @HackingTheCaseInterview, has millions of views.

Through my books, online courses, and coaching, I've helped thousands of students and working professionals land offers in consulting.

So, you can be confident that you'll be getting the very best information and guidance in this book.

How to Best Use This Book

This book is designed to be fast, practical, and immediately useful. Each lesson can be read in a few minutes, making it easy to squeeze in reading throughout your busy day.

You don't have to read the lessons in order. Feel free to skip around if you are interested in specific topics or if you already know where your knowledge gaps are.

This book is organized around 12 main sections:

- Profit
- Markets
- Customers
- Companies
- Competitive Advantage
- Products

- Pricing
- Operations
- Economics
- Mergers and acquisitions
- Financial statements and terms
- Industry primers

Whether you read this book cover to cover or just read a few sections, the key after learning a new concept is to ask yourself how you could apply it in an actual case interview.

This is exactly how you'll turn knowledge into instinct.

Without further ado, let's get started!

Taylor Warfield

2. Lessons on Profit

Overview

This section is all about profit, one of the most important and common measures of the health of a business. Everything a company does is ultimately aimed at increasing this number.

Here are the lessons that we'll cover:

- Profit
- Contribution margin
- Breakeven
- Increasing revenue
- Decreasing costs
- Gross profit
- Operating profit

- Net profit

- Profit margin

- Sales mix

Lesson #1: Profit

Profit is the difference between how much a business makes and how much it spends. It is the lifeblood of a business. It's what allows a business to survive and grow.

The basic formula for profit is:

Profit = Revenue – Costs

Example: Last month, a lemonade stand sold $1,000 of lemonade and had $200 of expenses. The lemonade stand made a profit of $800.

Let's take a look at revenue and costs more closely.

Revenue is all of the money a company brings in from selling its products and services. In most cases, revenue is calculated by multiplying the number of units sold by the price per unit.

Revenue = Quantity * Price

Example: If a lemonade stand sold 500 cups of lemonade at a price of $2 per cup, their revenue is $1,000.

Revenue is not profit because businesses still need to pay for everything that goes into producing and delivering their products and services.

That's where costs come in. In general, there are two types of costs: variable costs and fixed costs.

Variable costs are costs that change based on how much product is sold.

Example: Variable costs for a lemonade stand include:

- *Lemons*
- *Sugar*
- *Water*
- *Cups*
- *Ice*
- *Napkins*

The more lemonade that is sold, the more the business will need to spend on these things.

Fixed costs are costs that don't change based on how much product is sold.

Example: Fixed costs for a lemonade stand include:

- *Table*
- *Signage and decorations*
- *Pitchers*
- *Spoons*
- *Coolers*
- *Permits or licenses*

Generally, the lemonade stand will not need any more of these as they sell more lemonade.

So, we can now expand our equation for profit to look something like this:

Profit = (Quantity * Price) − Total Variable Costs − Fixed Costs

Profit = (Quantity * Price) − (Quantity * Variable Costs) − Fixed Costs

Profit = (Price − Variable Costs) * Quantity − Fixed Costs

Example: Suppose a lemonade stand sold 500 cups of lemonade at a price of $2 per cup. The variable costs are $0.75 per cup and fixed costs are $200.

What is the lemonade stand's profit?

*Profit = ($2 − $0.75) * 500 − $200*

Profit = $425

This lemonade stand made a profit of $425.

Not every business is profitable. Startups often spend more than they make in their earlier years while trying to grow quickly. Even larger companies sometimes operate at a loss if their costs rise unexpectedly or their sales drop.

In consulting case interviews, many of the problems you'll be asked to solve will involve fixing declining profits or figuring out ways to increase profit.

Lesson #2: Contribution Margin

Contribution margin measures how much money a business makes from selling a specific product or service. It helps businesses understand which products are actually worth selling.

The formula for contribution margin is:

Contribution Margin = Price − Variable Cost Per Unit

Example: Suppose a lemonade stand sells a cup of lemonade for $2. The variable costs to make one cup include:

- Lemons: $0.30

- Sugar: $0.10

- Water: $0.05

- Ice: $0.10

- Cup: $0.20

What is the contribution margin of a cup of lemonade?

The variable costs add up to a total of $0.75. Therefore, the contribution margin is $2 - $0.75 = $1.25.

This means that for each cup of lemonade sold, the business makes $1.25 from the sale.

However, remember that this is not necessarily all profit because the business still has fixed costs, such as the cost of the table, signage, cooler, and permits.

After all fixed costs are fully paid off, any remaining contribution margin becomes profit.

If a product has a high contribution margin, that means it's helping the company make money. If a product has a negative contribution margin, that means it's costing the company more to produce than it earns in sales.

In some cases, companies sell products at low or negative contribution margins on purpose, as part of a bigger strategy. They may do this to get new customers, who will hopefully also buy other products that have higher contribution margins.

Example #1: Businesses that manufacture printers often give away printers for free. These businesses lose money on the printers that they sell. However, they make their money back by selling ink cartridges, which typically have high contribution margins.

Example #2: Razors are typically priced low and have a low contribution margin. Razor blades, on the other hand, are expensive and have a high contribution margin.

Lesson #3: Breakeven

Every business wants to make a profit. Before they can do this, they need to cover all of their costs.

The point at which a business earns just enough revenue to cover its costs, but not yet make a profit is called the breakeven point.

In other words, breakeven happens when either:

- **Revenue = Costs**

- **Profit = $0**

Breakeven is important because it is the minimum performance a business needs just to survive. It's a key milestone.

Once a business reaches breakeven, every additional sale contributes directly to profit.

There are two ways to measure breakeven:

- **Breakeven quantity**: How many units a business needs to sell to cover all costs

- **Breakeven revenue**: How much total revenue a business needs to cover all costs

Breakeven quantity is what is most commonly asked for in consulting case interviews.

Here's how to calculate breakeven:

- **Breakeven Quantity = Fixed Costs ÷ Contribution Margin Per Unit**

- **Breakeven Revenue = Breakeven Quantity * Price**

Example: Suppose a lemonade stand sells lemonade at a price of $2 per cup. The variable costs are $0.75 per cup and fixed costs are $200.

What is the lemonade stand's breakeven quantity and breakeven revenue?

Contribution Margin = $2 - $0.75 = $1.25

Breakeven Quantity = $200 ÷ $1.25 = 160

The lemonade stand needs to sell 160 cups of lemonade to break even.

*Breakeven Revenue = 160 * $2 = $320*

The lemonade stand needs $320 in revenue to break even.

Businesses with high fixed costs and low variable costs, such as a software business, will have a higher breakeven point. However, they'll make more profit per sale after they reach breakeven.

Businesses with low fixed costs and high variable costs, such as a pop-up food stall, will have a lower breakeven point. However, they'll make less profit per sale afterwards.

Lesson #4: Increasing Revenue

When a business wants to increase its profit, there are two ways to get there: increase revenues or decrease costs.

Revenue is the starting point for any business. Without it, there's nothing to cover costs or generate profit. When a business wants to grow, one of the first questions it asks is: how can we increase revenue?

While there are many ways to grow revenue, they all fall into two main categories: organic growth and inorganic growth.

Let's break each of these down.

Organic growth

Organic growth means increasing revenue by improving or expanding what the business already does. This kind of growth comes from within the company itself. There are no mergers, acquisitions, or partnerships involved.

There are two types of organic growth:

1. Growth in existing revenue sources
2. Growth in new revenue sources

Growth in existing revenue sources means making more money from the same products or services the company already sells.

Here are a few ways to do this:

<u>Sell more units</u>

Example: A lemonade stand typically sells 500 cups per month. By staying open longer hours or promoting itself on social media, it can sell 600 cups.

<u>Raise prices</u>

Example: The lemonade stand could increase its price per cup from $2.00 to $2.50. If customers are willing to pay this, revenues will increase.

<u>Improve customer retention or repeat purchases</u>

Example: The lemonade stand could offer a "buy 5, get 1 free" punch card to encourage people to come back more often.

<u>Sell more to each customer</u>

Example: The lemonade stand could start offering a larger cup size and charge more for it.

All of these strategies don't require launching a new business or changing the product dramatically. They all focus on improving how the current business operates.

On the other hand, growth in new revenue sources means generating revenue from new products, services, or customer segments that the business wasn't targeting before.

Here are a few ways to do this:

Launching a new product

Example: The lemonade stand could start selling bottled lemonade or lemonade popsicles.

Expanding to new customer segments

Example: The lemonade stand could add sugar-free lemonade to appeal to health-conscious customers.

Entering new markets

Example: The lemonade stand could open a second location across town or start catering for local events.

New revenue sources often involve more risk and investment, but they can unlock big opportunities.

Inorganic growth

Inorganic growth happens when a company increases revenue by making an acquisition, merger, or partnership. This type of growth doesn't come from improving the company's own operations, but rather by buying growth.

Example: A lemonade stand could buy out another lemonade stand that is across the street. Now, it gets revenue from both locations.

Inorganic growth can quickly boost revenue and provide access to new customers, products, or capabilities.

However, it often comes with challenges, including merging operations, managing culture differences, and paying off the cost of the acquisition.

Lesson #5: Decreasing Costs

While many companies focus on increasing revenue to grow profits, controlling costs is just as important. This is especially important when revenue is flat or declining.

Remember that there are two types of costs that a business can try to reduce: variable costs and fixed costs. In general, decreasing variable costs is more achievable than trying to cut fixed costs.

Let's take a closer look at both.

Decreasing variable costs

Since variable costs are tied to production, they're often easier to reduce. Here are some common ways to do it:

Negotiate lower prices with suppliers

Example: The lemonade stand could find a wholesale supplier that sells lemons at a cheaper price per unit.

Buy in bulk

Example: Buying sugar in 10-pound bags instead of 1-pound bags may be cheaper per pound.

Reduce waste or inefficiency

Example: The lemonade stand might notice it's throwing away unused lemons at the end of each day. Better planning and storage could lower this waste.

Switch to cheaper ingredients

Example: This could be risky, but switching from fresh-squeezed lemons to a pre-mixed concentrate can cut costs if customers don't mind the change in taste.

Automate or simplify the process

Example: Using a faster juicer might let one person handle more orders, reducing the need to hire extra help.

Small reductions in variable costs can add up quickly, especially for high-volume businesses.

Decreasing fixed costs

Since fixed costs are often tied to long-term investments or contracts, they're harder to reduce. Changes usually take longer to implement.

Still, some options for lowering fixed costs include:

Downsizing or relocating

Example: A lemonade stand might move to a different city where business permits are cheaper.

Outsourcing

Example: Instead of buying a juicer and hiring someone to juice the lemons, the business could pay a local juice supplier to deliver fresh lemonade concentrate.

Cutting non-essential spending

Example: If the lemonade stand spent $50 on fancy signage, it could switch to cheaper homemade signs next season.

<u>Sharing resources</u>

Example: Two lemonade stands might share a storage cooler or jointly apply for a permit.

Because fixed costs tend to be locked in for a long period of time, businesses are usually more successful and flexible when focusing on lowering variable costs first.

Lesson #6: Gross Profit

Profit isn't just one number. There are different types of profit that measure different aspects of a business's health. In this lesson, we're going to take a closer look at gross profit.

Gross profit measures the money a business earns from selling its products or services after subtracting the costs to produce and sell them.

In other words, it is a measure of how efficiently a business produces what it sells.

The formula for gross profit is:

Gross Profit = Revenue – Cost of Goods Sold

Let's break this down.

Recall that revenue is the total money the company brings in from selling its products and services.

Cost of goods sold, also known as COGS for short, is the total of all the variable costs required to make and deliver the product or service.

These are the same kinds of variable costs we talked about in earlier lessons, which includes materials, labor, packaging, and shipping.

COGS does not include fixed costs, such as equipment, rent, or advertising.

Example: Suppose a lemonade stand sells 500 cups of lemonade at $2 each. The cost of goods sold includes the costs of lemons, sugar, water, ice, and cups and totals $0.75.

*Revenue = 500 * $2 = $1,000*

*COGS = 500 * $0.75 = $375*

Gross Profit = $1,000 - $375 - $625

$625 is what the business has left after covering the direct costs of making and serving the lemonade, but before paying for things such as signage, permits, or any marketing expenses.

Gross profit is a quick way to see if a business's core business model makes sense. If the gross profit is low or negative, that may mean:

- Prices are too low

- Variable costs are too high

Businesses aim for a healthy gross profit so they have enough money left over to cover fixed costs and make an overall profit.

Lesson #7: Operating Profit

After covering the cost of producing and selling a product, a business still has many other expenses to pay. These include equipment, rent, and marketing.

Operating profit shows how much money is left after paying for all day-to-day business operations, but before any interest and taxes.

It's one of the most important measures of a company's financial health, because it reflects the core strength of the business and how well it performs from running its regular operations.

The formula for operating profit is:

Operating Profit = Gross Profit – Operating Expenses

Operating expenses are the costs required to run the business, other than the direct costs of producing the product. These can include:

- Rent for retail or office space
- Salaries for staff (not directly involved in production)
- Marketing and advertising
- Utilities (e.g., electricity, water, internet)
- Insurance
- Equipment maintenance

Operating profit is sometimes called EBIT, which stands for Earnings Before Interest and Taxes.

This is the number many investors and analysts look at to judge how well a company's core operations are performing without being affected by financing choices or tax strategies.

Example: Let's return to our example on a lemonade stand. Recall that they have:

- *Revenue = $1,000*
- *COGS = $375*
- *Gross Profit = $625*

Suppose they have the following operating expenses:

- *Table rental: $100*

- Permits and licenses: $50

- Advertising flyers: $50

- Cooler rental: $50

Total Operating Expenses = $250

Operating Profit = $625 − $250 = $375

This means that the lemonade stand made $375 from its business operations after paying both variable and fixed costs.

Operating profit is a key indicator of how efficiently a company runs its business. It answers the question: is this business model working once we account for all the typical costs of running it?

A company can have high revenue and high gross profit, but still have low or negative operating profit if its operating expenses are out of control.

If operating profit is declining while gross profit is healthy, it might be due to:

- Rising marketing costs

- Rising rent costs

- Inefficient staffing

- Poor management of overhead costs (e.g., utilities, insurance, equipment maintenance)

Lesson #8: Net Profit

Net profit is the final profit a business earns after subtracting all of its expenses from its revenue. It's often called the bottom line because it appears at the bottom of a company's income statement.

We'll cover financial statements later on, so don't worry about what an income statement is for now.

Net profit shows the total amount of money the business keeps after paying for:

- Cost of goods sold (COGS)
- Operating expenses
- Interest on debt
- Taxes

It is the most complete measure of a business's profitability. It includes every cost the business has to pay, so what's left over is what the business can actually use to pay owners, reinvest in growth, or build savings.

The formula for net profit is:

Net Profit = Revenue – All Expenses

Example: Let's revisit our lemonade stand again.

- Revenue = $1,000
- COGS = $375
- Operating expenses = $250
- Interest on a loan = $100
- Taxes = $100

What is the lemonade stand's net profit?

Gross Profit = $1,000 - $375 = $625

Operating Profit = $625 - $250 = $375

Net Profit = $375 - $100 - $100 = $175

So, the lemonade stand made $175 in net profit.

Lesson #9: Profit Margin

Profit margin is one of the most common ways to evaluate how efficiently a business turns its revenue into profit. Profit margin is also referred to as profitability.

Rather than looking at just the dollar amount of profit, profit margin shows profit as a percentage of revenue. This makes it easier to compare businesses of different sizes.

The formula for profit margin is:

Profit Margin = (Profit ÷ Revenue) × 100%

Example: Suppose our lemonade stand has revenues of $1,000 and a profit of $175. What is its profit margin?

Profit Margin = ($175 ÷ $1,000) × 100% = 17.5%

This means that for every $1 the lemonade stand earns in revenue, it keeps 17.5 cents as profit.

Profit margin can be calculated for the different types of profit that we covered:

- Gross profit margin
- Operating profit margin
- Net profit margin

These formulas are what you would expect:

- **Gross Margin = (Gross Profit ÷ Revenue) × 100%**

- **Operating Margin = (Operating Profit ÷ Revenue) × 100%**

- **Net Profit Margin = (Net Profit ÷ Revenue) × 100%**

Example: Continuing with our example on a lemonade stand, recall that we had the following information:

- *Revenue = $1,000*

- *COGS = $375*

- *Operating expenses = $250*

- *Interest on a loan = $100*

- *Taxes = $100*

Gross Margin = ($625 ÷ $1,000) × 100% = 62.5%

Operating Margin = ($375 ÷ $1,000) × 100% = 37.5%

Net Profit Margin = ($175 ÷ $1,000) × 100% = 17.5%

Lesson #10: Sales Mix

Sales mix, also called product mix, is the relative proportion of different products or services that a company sells within a given time period.

It represents the breakdown of total revenue across the company's various products and services.

Example: A coffee shop sells 50 drinks per day consisting of:

- *25 lattes*

- *15 regular coffees*

- 10 specialty drinks

Based on this, what is their sales mix?

The sales mix at this coffee shop is 50% lattes, 30% regular coffees, and 20% specialty drinks.

Sales mix is important because it directly impacts the company's overall profitability since different products can have different profit margins.

Even if total revenue is the same, a company's overall profitability could decline if sales mix changes.

A shift toward more sales of higher-margin products improves profitability while a shift toward more sales of lower-margin products reduces profitability.

Example: A software company sells basic licenses and premium licenses.

- Basic licenses have a profit margin of 20%

- Premium licenses have a profit margin of 60%

If the company changes from a 50%/50% split of basic/premium to a 70%/30% split of basic/premium, how do overall profit margins change?

- Profit Margin (50/50 split) = (50% * 20%) + (50% * 60%) = 40%

- Profit Margin (70/30 split) = (70% * 20%) + (30% * 60%) = 32%

The profit margin decreases from 40% to 32% because of the change in sales mix.

Successful companies actively manage their sales mix through a combination of strategic pricing and incentives that guide customers toward higher-margin products.

The key is to make it easier and more attractive for customers to choose more profitable products.

3. Lessons on Markets

Overview

This section is all about markets, the collective group of potential buyers for a specific product or service.

Here are the lessons that we'll cover:

- Market size
- Market growth rate
- Market share
- Relative market share
- Fragmented vs. concentrated market
- Ways to enter a market
- Barriers to entry
- Supply chain

- Vertical integration

- Bargaining power

- Porter's Five Forces

Lesson #11: Market Size

Market size is a measure of how big a particular market is. It tells you how much money all customers together spend. In other words, knowing the market size answers the question: how large is the business opportunity?

Understanding market size helps businesses decide whether an opportunity is worth pursuing.

Example: A business with $10B in annual revenue will probably be more interested in entering a new market that has a size of $10B than a new market with a size of $10M.

Entering a $10B market gives the business an opportunity to increase revenue by 100%. On the other hand, entering a $10M market only gives the business an opportunity to increase revenue by 0.1%.

In consulting case interviews, you may be asked to calculate the size of a particular market. The most straight forward way to do this is by using the formula:

Market Size = Total Customers × Average Spend per Customer

Example: Calculate the market size of sneakers in the United States.

To calculate this, let's start by assuming the U.S. population is about 350 million people. Let's assume that 80% of people purchase sneakers. That means there are 280 million customers.

Let's assume that a person buys 2 pairs of sneakers a year. Suppose the average price of a pair of sneakers is $75. So, the average spend per customer is $150.

Market Size = 280 million × $150 = $42 billion

The market size for sneakers in the United States is roughly $42 billion.

Lesson #12: Market Growth Rate

A market size is important, but just as important is how fast that market is growing. A growing market creates more opportunities while a shrinking market may signal trouble ahead.

A market that is growing quickly is more attractive than a market that is flat or shrinking. Businesses in fast growing markets can gain more customers and increase revenue more easily.

To measure market growth over time, we use something called the Compound Annual Growth Rate, also known as CAGR for short.

CAGR is the annual growth rate of a market or business over a period of time, assuming the growth happened steadily each year.

The formula for CAGR is a bit complicated and you'll most likely never need to calculate it during a case interview. However, you should be familiar with seeing it.

$$CAGR = (\text{Ending Value} / \text{Beginning Value})^{1/\text{Number of Years}} - 1$$

Example: The global sneaker market was $60 billion five years ago. Now it is $100 billion. What is the global sneaker market's average growth rate over this time period?

$$CAGR = (\$100 \text{ billion} / \$60 \text{ billion})^{1/5} - 1$$

$$CAGR \approx 0.108$$

The sneaker market grew by 10.8% per year on average over the past 5 years.

Lesson #13: Market Share

Market share is a way of measuring how much of a market a business controls. It helps businesses understand how they compare to competitors.

The higher a company's market share, the more dominant it is in that market. A company with growing market share is gaining ground, while a company with shrinking market share may be falling behind.

Market share is often used to evaluate competitive positioning, identify room for growth, and analyze changes in the market over time.

The formula for market share is simple:

Market Share = Company Revenue ÷ Total Market Revenue

Market share is usually expressed as a percentage.

Example: Suppose a sneaker company earns $60 billion in revenue per year and the total global sneaker market size is $100 billion.

Market Share = $60 billion ÷ $100 billion

Market Share = 60%

The sneaker company has 60% market share, which means they are the market leader.

Lesson #14: Relative Market Share

While market share tells you how much of the market a business owns overall, relative market share tells you how that business stacks up against the biggest competitor.

Relative market share is a way to measure competitive strength in a market. The formula for relative market share is:

Relative Market Share = Market Share / Largest Competitor's Market Share

Relative market share is typically expressed as a ratio, not a percentage.

A relative market share greater than 1 implies that the business is the market leader. The number shows how much larger the business is compared to the next largest player.

Example: Your sneaker company has a 60% market share. The largest competitor has a market share of 20%.

Relative Market Share = 60% / 20% = 3

A relative market share of 3 means that your business is three times the size of the next largest player.

A relative market share that is less than 1 implies that the business is not the market leader. The number shows how close they are to being tied for market leadership.

Example: Your sneaker company has a 20% market share. The largest competitor has a market share of 40%.

Relative Market Share = 20% / 40% = 0.5

A relative market share of 0.5 means that your business is half the size of the market leader.

Another reason why relative market share is useful is because market share by itself may not reveal the true competitiveness of a market.

Example: If a company has a 10% market share, is that good or bad?

The answer depends on the layout of the market.

If the market leader has an 80% market share, then a 10% market share means the business is significantly behind its competitor.

However, if the business has a 10% market share and the next largest player has a 1% market share, that means that the business is significantly ahead of its competition.

Lesson #15: Fragmented vs. Concentrated Market

Markets can look very different depending on how many businesses compete in them and how much market share each business holds. Two common ways to describe a market are either a fragmented market or a concentrated market.

Understanding the difference between these two types of markets will help you analyze competition and spot opportunities in a case interview.

Fragmented market

A fragmented market is one where no single company dominates. Instead, many small or mid-sized competitors share the market.

Characteristics of a fragmented market:

- No player has a large market share
- Easy for new competitors to enter the market
- Lots of customer choice
- Often very price-competitive
- Hard to build strong brand recognition

Example: A market that has 1,000 businesses with each business having no more than 1% market share would be considered a highly fragmented market.

Markets that are typically fragmented include:

- Home services
- Real estate
- Restaurants
- Freelance services
- Fitness and wellness
- Private education and tutoring
- Beauty and personal care

The main advantage of entering a fragmented market is that it is easier to enter and there are more opportunities to grow. However, it'll be harder to gain customer loyalty and there will be a lot of pricing pressure.

Concentrated market

A concentrated market is one where a few large companies dominate most of the market share.

Characteristics of a concentrated market:

- High market share held by top players
- Hard for new competitors to enter the market
- More pricing power
- Less innovation

Example: A market that has two businesses that have a combined market share of 90% would be considered a highly concentrated market.

Markets that are typically concentrated include:

- Oil and gas
- Aircraft manufacturing
- Telecommunications
- Package delivery
- Automobile manufacturing
- Technology platforms
- Smartphones

The main advantage of entering a concentrated market is higher profit margins and more control over pricing. However, it'll be difficult to break into the market and there won't be much opportunity for growth.

Lesson #16: Ways to Enter a Market

When a business wants to expand into a new market, whether it's a new country, a new customer segment, or a new product area, it has three main options:

1. Build from scratch
2. Partnership
3. Joint venture

Each approach has its advantages and disadvantages. The right choice depends on factors such as speed, control, cost, and expertise.

It's helpful to ask the following questions:

- Does the business want to move fast or do they want full control?

- How much is the business willing to invest?

- How much expertise and understanding does the business have of the new market?

Let's dive deeper into the three ways to enter a market.

1. Build from scratch

Entering a market by building from scratch means a business is doing everything on its own. The business will build the product, hire the team, set up operations, and market directly to customers.

Advantages:

- Full control over branding, pricing, and operations

- Business keeps 100% of profits

- Builds long-term internal capabilities

Disadvantages:

- Slower to launch

- Requires a lot of upfront investment

- Higher risk if the business doesn't understand the market well

Building from scratch works best when the business has deep experience, strong resources, and confidence in its ability to do everything on its own.

2. Partnership

A partnership means working with an existing business in an informal or flexible way, without forming a new legal entity together.

Advantages:

- Faster market access
- Lower investment than building from scratch
- Leverages partner's customer base and experience

Disadvantages:

- Less control over branding, pricing, and operations
- Potential for misaligned goals
- Risk of being dependent on the partner

Partnerships are good for testing new markets without committing too much money or time upfront.

3. Joint venture

A joint venture is when two companies form a new, shared business entity to enter a market together. Both companies contribute resources, share control, and split profits.

Advantages:

- Greater commitment than a partnership
- Shared cost and risk
- Combines strengths of both companies

Disadvantages:

- Legal and financial complexity
- Less control over branding, pricing, and operations
- Potential conflict over decision-making

Lesson #17: Barriers to Entry

When a company considers entering a new market, one of the first things it needs to understand are the barriers to entry. Barriers to entry are the obstacles that make it difficult for new businesses to enter a market and compete effectively.

The higher the barriers, the harder it is to break in. The lower the barriers, the easier it is for new competitors to enter.

Examples of common barriers to entry include:

- High startup costs
- Strong brand loyalty
- Scale
- Legal or regulatory requirements
- Technology or intellectual property
- Network effects
- Access to suppliers
- Access to distribution channels

High startup costs

Some markets require a lot of money upfront to get started. These high startup costs might include equipment, real estate, technology, research and development, or staffing.

Due to these costs, only companies with substantial financial resources or access to funding can realistically compete.

Example: Starting an airline company requires purchasing or leasing aircraft, hiring pilots and crew, maintaining aircraft, and securing airport slots. These upfront costs can easily reach hundreds of millions of dollars.

Strong brand loyalty

In many industries, consumers develop deep trust and familiarity with certain brands over time. These brands often have strong reputations for quality, consistency, or customer service, which can lead to customer loyalty.

This makes it hard for new entrants to convince customers to try their products, even if they are cheaper or better.

Example: People are more likely to buy Coke or Pepsi than a new soda brand they've never heard of because they know what to expect and associate the brands with quality and trust.

Scale

Larger companies benefit from something called economies of scale, which is when their average costs go down as their production goes up.

This allows them to sell products at lower prices while maintaining profitability, something new or small companies may not be able to match.

In addition to cost advantages, scale can bring other benefits such as better logistics, greater marketing reach, and stronger negotiating power with suppliers and distributors.

Example: Amazon serves millions of customers globally. To support this, it has built an extensive network of fulfillment centers, uses automated systems, and negotiates low shipping rates. All of this gives it major cost and speed advantages over smaller online retailers.

We'll cover this topic in more detail in a later lesson.

Legal or regulatory requirements

Certain markets are heavily regulated due to safety, financial, or ethical concerns. Companies may need government approval, licenses, or certifications to operate legally.

Navigating this regulatory environment can be time-consuming and costly, creating a high barrier for new entrants.

Example: Starting a bank or other financial institution requires regulatory approval, meeting minimum capital requirements, implementing strict security protocols, and following complex financial laws.

Technology or intellectual property

When a company owns critical technology or intellectual property, it can prevent others from copying or replicating its products.

This gives the company a legal monopoly over certain features or innovations, protecting it from competition for a period of time.

Example: Apple's iPhone includes patented hardware designs and software features. These patents protect Apple from competitors directly copying their innovations, forcing competitors to spend more time and money developing alternatives.

We'll cover this topic in more detail in a later lesson.

Network effects

Some businesses become more valuable as more people use them. This is known as the network effect and it's especially common in technology and platform-based businesses.

This creates a self-reinforcing loop.

New entrants struggle because they start with few users and customers often prefer platforms that already have a large, active user base.

Example: Social media platforms like Instagram or LinkedIn are difficult to disrupt because users go where their friends, colleagues, or audiences already are. A new platform with no users offers little value to someone considering switching.

We'll cover this topic in more detail in a later lesson.

Access to suppliers

In many industries, especially those with specialized inputs or materials, having access to reliable suppliers is critical. Existing companies often have long-standing contracts, exclusive deals, or preferred customer status with key suppliers.

This can make it difficult for new entrants to source essential materials at competitive prices or even at all.

Example: In the automotive industry, large manufacturers often have decades-long relationships with parts suppliers. A new startup may struggle to secure components such as batteries or semiconductors.

Access to distribution channels

Getting products into the hands of customers is a major hurdle for new businesses. In many markets, established players already dominate prime distribution channels.

This includes shelf space in retailers, partnerships with online marketplaces, or direct relationships with distributors.

Example: In the beverage industry, Coca-Cola has exclusive agreements with restaurants, vending machines, and stadiums, leaving little room for other competitors to gain market share.

Lesson #18: Supply Chain

Every product you buy goes through a supply chain.

A supply chain is the full journey a product takes to get from raw materials all the way to the customer. It includes all the people, companies, and steps involved in producing, moving, and selling that product.

Understanding the supply chain is important because problems at any step can affect a company's ability to operate and make a profit.

A strong supply chain helps a company produce high-quality products, deliver products on time, control costs, and respond quickly to demand.

A weak supply chain could mean empty shelves, expensive delays, or poor customer reviews.

Let's discuss the key parts of a typical supply chain:

1. Supplier
2. Manufacturer
3. Distributor
4. Retailer
5. Customer

1. Supplier

Suppliers are the starting point in a supply chain. They provide the raw materials needed to make a product.

Example: To manufacture sneakers, a company will need to source rubber for soles, fabric for the upper part of the shoe, foam for cushioning, and plastic or metal for eyelets and logos.

2. Manufacturer

Manufacturers take raw materials and turn them into finished products.

Example: A factory is contracted to cut fabric, mold soles, stitch everything together, and package the sneakers for shipping.

3. Distributor

Distributors move products in bulk from manufacturers to retailers or other businesses. They help with storage, transportation, and logistics.

Example: Sneakers might be shipped in containers to warehouses in North America, Europe, or Asia, where they're stored and later sent to stores.

4. Retailer

Retailers are the final stop before the customer. They sell directly to consumers. Retailers don't make or transport the product, but focus on selling it.

Example: For sneakers, retailers could include sporting goods stores, department stores, or online stores.

5. Customer

The end of the supply chain is the customer, who buys and uses the product.

Example: When a customer walks into a store and purchases their sneakers, the supply chain is complete.

Lesson #19: Vertical Integration

Vertical integration is when a company expands its control over more steps in its own supply chain. It is called "vertical" because the supply chain is often visualized as a vertical stack of different stages:

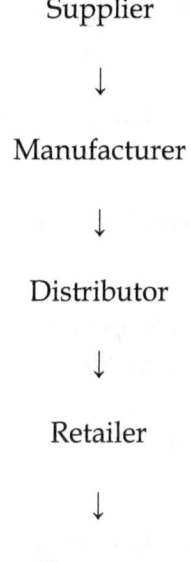

Supplier
↓
Manufacturer
↓
Distributor
↓
Retailer
↓
Customer

Instead of relying on third parties, a company may choose to bring in more parts of the manufacturing or distribution process in-house.

Example: A fully vertically integrated shoe company would do all of the following:

- *Source its own raw materials*
- *Manufacture sneakers in a company-owned factory*
- *Ship products through its own distribution centers*
- *Sell directly to customers through its own branded stores and website*

There are two types of vertical integration:

- Backward integration
- Forward integration

Backward integration means taking over steps earlier in the supply chain.

Example: A shoe company buys a rubber supplier so it can make its own soles instead of purchasing from someone else.

Forward integration means taking over steps later in the supply chain.

Example: The same shoe company opens its own stores or builds its own e-commerce website instead of selling through third-party retailers.

There are many reasons why a company might choose to vertically integrate:

- More control over quality, costs, and timelines
- Higher profit margins by cutting out the middleman
- Better coordination across the supply chain
- Competitive advantage if other companies can't replicate it

However, vertical integration does have some downsides:

- High costs to build and maintain
- Reduces flexibility of switching partners or pivoting quickly
- Can become inefficient if the company tries to do too much

In deciding whether it makes sense for a company to vertically integrate, you'll need to weigh the cost, control, and risk trade-offs. Sometimes, sticking with using third parties may be better.

Lesson #20: Bargaining Power

Bargaining power is a company's ability to influence the terms of a deal when working with suppliers, manufacturers, distributors, or customers. This might include:

- Pricing
- Quality
- Delivery time
- Contract length

If a company has high bargaining power, they can demand better prices or contract terms. If a company has low bargaining power, they may have to accept what the other side offers.

There are two types of relationships where bargaining power often matters most:

1. Bargaining power of suppliers
2. Bargaining power of buyers

There are a number of different factors that influence how much bargaining power a company has:

- Number of alternatives
- Switching costs
- Volume and importance
- Differentiation and uniqueness

Number of alternatives

The more choices one side has, the stronger their position.

Example #1: If your sneaker company can buy rubber soles from 20 different suppliers, none of them have much power over you because you can always switch to another supplier.

However, if there is only 1 rubber sole supplier, they'll have much more power over you since they know you don't have any other options.

Example #2: If you sell only through one giant retailer and they threaten to drop you, they hold the power.

However, if you sell through dozens of retailers or directly to customers, no single buyer can control you.

Switching costs

Switching costs are how hard or expensive it is to change suppliers or buyers.

Example: If switching rubber suppliers would require redesigning the sole and testing new materials, the supplier has more bargaining power because they know that it's expensive and inconvenient for you to switch suppliers.

Volume and importance

Whichever side represents more business for the other usually has more bargaining power.

Example: If your sneaker company buys 50% of a small supplier's total output, they'll do a lot to keep your business. However, if you're just 1% of their total sales, they may not care much if you leave.

Differentiation and uniqueness

If one side offers something truly unique or hard to replicate, they hold more bargaining power.

Example: If you use a specific type of foam cushioning in your sneakers that only one supplier can make, they have more bargaining power. They know you can't just go and work with any other supplier.

Lesson #21: Porter's Five Forces

Porter's Five Forces is one of the most widely used frameworks to help businesses understand the competitive pressures in a market. It was originally created by Harvard professor Michael Porter.

The more intense these forces are, the harder it is to be profitable. The weaker the forces are, the more attractive the industry.

The five forces are:

1. Competitive rivalry
2. Threat of new entrants
3. Threat of substitutes
4. Bargaining power of suppliers
5. Bargaining power of buyers

1. Competitive rivalry

Competitive rivalry looks at how intense the competition is among existing companies in the industry.

If there are many competitors that are all fighting for the same customers, prices can get pushed down and profits will shrink.

However, if there are only a few companies that dominate the market and they don't compete too aggressively, profits tend to be higher.

Example #1: In the fast-food industry, McDonald's, Burger King, Wendy's, and many more chains are constantly competing with each other. So, rivalry is high.

Example #2: In airplane manufacturing, Boeing and Airbus are the only companies that manufacture commercial airplanes. So, while there is rivalry between the two, it is just limited to two major players.

2. Threat of new entrants

Threat of new entrants looks at how easy it is for new companies to enter the industry and become competitors.

If there are low barriers to entry, new competitors can show up and reduce profits for everyone else. If there are high barriers to entry, existing companies are more protected.

Example #1: Starting a lemonade stand is easy. Anyone can join in, so the threat of new entrants is high.

Example #2: Entering the airline industry is extremely difficult due to high costs and regulations. So, the threat of new entrants is low.

3. Threat of substitutes

Threat of substitutes looks at whether customers can switch to a different product that solves the same problem.

If many substitutes exist, your product can be replaced. So, you'll be pressured to lower prices or improve quality to compete with these substitutes.

On the other hand, if there are few or no good substitutes, you have much more pricing power.

Example #1: For a soda company, there are many substitutes to their product. Customers could consume water, juice, coffee, and energy drinks instead of soda. Therefore, the threat of substitutes is high.

Example #2: There may be few or no substitutes for prescription medicine. So, the threat of substitutes is low.

4. Bargaining power of suppliers

This force looks at how much power suppliers have over a business.

If there are only a few suppliers, then suppliers can demand higher prices because there aren't too many different suppliers to choose from.

However, if there are many suppliers, then suppliers have less power since you have so many different suppliers competing for your business.

Example: If you run a cafe and only one local bakery sells the special bread you use, then they can raise prices more easily. However, if dozens of bakeries can supply you with similar bread, then you will have more negotiating power to get better prices.

5. Bargaining power of buyers

This force looks at how much power customers have over a business.

If customers have many choices and can easily switch to a competitor, then they have more power. However, if your product is unique or switching is hard, your customers will have less power.

Example #1: If you sell basic t-shirts online, customers can easily shop elsewhere. Buyer power is high. If your prices are too high, customers won't purchase from you.

Example #2: If you're the only clinic in town that offers a specialized medical procedure, then buyer power is low. Customers will most likely pay whatever price you set.

Summary

To wrap up this lesson, let's review what makes a market attractive and unattractive.

Characteristics of an attractive market

- Low competitive rivalry
- Low threat of new entrants

- Low threat of substitutes
- Low bargaining power of suppliers
- Low bargaining power of buyers

Characteristics of an unattractive market

- High competitive rivalry
- High threat of new entrants
- High threat of substitutes
- High bargaining power of suppliers
- High bargaining power of buyers

4. Lessons on Customers

Overview

This section is all about customers. Without customers, businesses won't survive. These lessons will help you better understand customer needs and purchasing behavior.

Here are the lessons that we'll cover:

- Customer segmentation
- Customer acquisition cost
- Customer lifetime value
- Customer sales funnel
- Loss aversion
- Price anchoring
- Paradox of choice

- Decoy effect
- Psychological pricing
- Default bias
- Scarcity

Lesson #22: Customer Segmentation

Not all customers are the same. They don't all want the same things, respond to the same ads, or pay the same price.

That's why businesses use something called customer segmentation, which is the practice of grouping customers based on shared characteristics so they can better serve them.

Instead of treating everyone the same, companies create different strategies for each customer group.

Customers can be segmented based on things like:

- Demographics (e.g., age, gender, income)
- Psychographics (e.g., values, interests, lifestyle)
- Geography
- Behavior
- Needs or use cases

Specifically, segmentation helps companies:

- Tailor marketing to different groups
- Improve product offerings by focusing on specific needs

- Set smarter pricing since some segments will pay more than others

- Increase profitability by matching products with the right customers

Example: Suppose that an online streaming service decides to go after all customers in a market with the same strategy. They may only be able to capture 10% of the market.

Instead, if that company focuses on a specific customer segment, they can do a better job acquiring and retaining those specific customers.

Different customer segments that they could go after include:

Families

- *Want kid-friendly content and parental controls*

- *Value animated shows, educational content, and ad-free experiences*

- *Often use the same account across multiple devices*

Binge watchers

- *Watch full seasons of shows in days*

- *Love drama, thrillers, and reality TV*

- *Value auto-play features and smart recommendations*

International viewers

- *Prefer content in local languages or with subtitles*

- *Have different content preferences and cultural tastes*

- *Often underserved by content libraries centered around the U.S.*

Budget-conscious users

- *Want lower-cost, ad-supported plans*
- *Will cancel quickly if they don't feel it's worth it*
- *Respond well to bundle deals, discounts, and promotions*

Suppose that this company goes after families, which make up 30% of the market. They may be able to capture 60% of that segment by investing in product features that families care about and developing tailored marketing materials to that segment.

By doing this, they'll end up with 18% market share instead of the 10% market share they would have had if they went after all customers without doing any customer segmentation.

The key takeaway of this lesson is that if you try to serve everyone the same way, you usually end up serving no one particularly well.

Lesson #23: Customer Acquisition Cost

Every business needs customers. However, customers don't just appear. Businesses need to spend money to acquire customers.

An important metric that businesses keep track of is their customer acquisition cost or CAC for short.

Customer acquisition cost tells you how much it costs to acquire one new customer. This includes all money a company spends on:

- Online ads
- TV or radio commercials
- Influencer marketing
- Referral bonuses

- Sales team salaries and commissions

If money is spent to get a customer, it counts towards the customer acquisition cost.

CAC helps a company understand how efficient and sustainable their growth is.

If a business spends more to get customers than it earns from them, it loses money. But if it can get customers cheaply and keep them coming back, it makes money.

Knowing CAC also helps companies:

- Set smart marketing budgets

- Compare the performance of different marketing channels

- Decide whether to spend more to grow faster

- Evaluate profitability and pricing strategies

Example: Imagine you're running an online streaming service. To attract new customers, you spend $2 million on online ads. As a result, 200,000 new customers sign up and start paying.

Customer acquisition cost = $2 million / 200,000 = $10

This means it costs you $10 to acquire each paying customer.

Lesson #24: Customer Lifetime Value

Not all customers are equally valuable.

Some might only purchase once from your company and never be seen again. Others might stick around for years or even the rest of their lives.

Customer lifetime value, or LTV, is a way to measure how much a business can expect to earn from a customer over the entire time they stay a customer.

It is one of the most important metrics that businesses keep track of, especially for subscription-based companies.

The basic formula for customer lifetime value is:

LTV = Average Customer Lifespan × Average Revenue Per Month

Example: An online streaming service has an average customer lifespan of 12 months. Customers pay $10 per month for the service. What is the average customer lifetime value?

*LTV = 12 * $10 = $120*

The average customer lifetime value is $120.

Customer lifetime value helps companies understand how valuable their customers are and how much they can afford to spend to get them.

Example: If a customer is worth $120 over their lifetime, then spending $10 to acquire them is a great use of money. On the other hand, if a customer is only worth $5 over their lifetime, then spending $10 to acquire them is probably a losing strategy.

LTV also helps companies prioritize high-value customer segments, forecast long-term revenue, and make decisions on pricing and retention strategies.

Lesson #25: Customer Sales Funnel

Before someone becomes a paying customer, they go through a journey. They'll first hear about a company, think about them, try them out, and hopefully stick around.

This journey is often called a customer sales funnel because it starts with lots of potential customers at the top and narrows down to the few who actually buy and stay.

The customer sales funnel helps businesses understand how customers make decisions and where they might be dropping off. It's especially useful for improving marketing, sales, and retention strategies.

There are many versions of the customer sales funnel, but most follow four key steps:

1. Awareness
2. Consideration
3. Conversion
4. Retention

Let's go through each step in more detail.

1. Awareness

Awareness is when potential customers first learn that your company exists. They're not ready to purchase from you yet.

Companies use advertising, social media, and partnerships to build awareness.

Example: A college student sees a YouTube ad for a streaming service while watching a video. Now they're aware of this brand, even if they don't click or sign up right away.

2. Consideration

At this stage, the person knows about your company and is thinking about whether to try it. They might compare you to competitors, read reviews, or ask friends.

Companies try to stand out at this stage through good messaging, strong features, and trust-building content.

Example: The college student visits the company's website, browses their movie selection, reads a blog post about their original shows, and watches a few trailers. They're curious, but still haven't signed up yet.

3. Conversion

This is when the person takes action and becomes a paying customer. It could mean signing up, subscribing, or making a purchase depending on what the business model is.

Improving this stage often involves simplifying sign-ups or checkouts and offering free trials or promotions.

Example: After a few days, the college student sees an Instagram ad offering a free 30-day trial. They sign up and start watching. That's a conversion.

4. Retention

Getting a customer isn't the end of the customer sales funnel. Companies want customers to stick around and keep buying. This is the retention stage.

Retention strategies include customer loyalty programs, customer support, and personalized experiences.

Example: The company keeps the student engaged with weekly emails about new releases and personalized recommendations. The student enjoys the content and decides to stay subscribed after the free trial ends.

The customer sales funnel is useful because it helps companies:

- Identify where customers are dropping off and focus efforts on weak spots

- Align marketing, sales, and product teams around the same goals

- Increase revenue by improving conversion and retention rates

Many businesses focus too much on just getting more people into the funnel. The real value often comes from improving each stage, especially turning existing customers into loyal, long-term users.

Lesson #26: Loss Aversion

Customers don't always make rational decisions. In fact, they rarely do, especially when it comes to spending money.

Customers are influenced by emotion, habits, and subconscious biases. That's why understanding customer psychology is so powerful in business.

Companies that can understand how customers think, feel, and behave can design better products, set smarter prices, and create more effective marketing.

In this lesson, we'll cover the first of many psychological concepts that influence customer decisions.

Loss Aversion

People are more motivated to avoid losing something than to gain something of equal value. This is known as loss aversion.

Losing $10 feels more painful than gaining $10 feels good even though the dollar amount is the same in both scenarios.

People will go to greater lengths to avoid losses than to achieve gains. A study found that on average, the pain of a loss is about 2x stronger than the pleasure of a gain.

So, if you frame your message around what the customer might lose, they're more likely to take action.

Example #1: Imagine a streaming service is considering sending one of two different messages to new customers before their free trial ends:

- *"You're about to lose access to your favorite shows"*

- *"Upgrade now to continue watching"*

The first message creates urgency and a fear of loss.

The second message doesn't hit as hard. It doesn't emphasize the loss but instead talks about what the customer has to gain.

To get more customers to continue their subscription, the first message will probably work better for the majority of people.

Example #2: People tend to overpay for extended warranties or unnecessary insurance because they overestimate the pain they'd feel if something went wrong.

Lesson #27: Price Anchoring

People often don't know what something should cost. So, they look at the first price they see and use it as a mental benchmark. This first number is called the anchor.

Once an anchor is set, it shapes how people view everything else.

Companies use price anchoring to make a product look like a better deal by showing a higher-priced alternative first.

Example #1: Imagine you walk into a store and see a shirt priced at $200. Later, you see a similar shirt priced for $100. Suddenly, the $100 shirt feels like a great deal even if it's still overpriced.

This happens because the $200 shirt set the price anchor.

Example #2: Imagine walking into a store and seeing a $150 shirt that is marked down to $75. This makes $75 feel cheap compared to the anchor even if $75 was the intended price all along.

Price anchors don't have to be realistic. They just need to be the first thing that's seen.

Lesson #28: Paradox of Choice

You might think that more choices mean more sales, but too many options can actually overwhelm customers and cause them to walk away.

Too many options can make customers anxious, indecisive, and decision-making less satisfying. This is called the paradox of choice.

Example #1: A streaming service with hundreds of shows but no personalized recommendations might frustrate users. Users may end up scrolling endlessly, watching nothing, and feeling disappointed.

Example #2: Imagine you go to the store to buy a bottle of shampoo and see 40 options. There are different bottles with different brands, scents, formulas, and sizes.

You might spend 20 minutes reading labels, walk away with nothing, or purchase something and then second-guess your choice all day.

Instead, if there were only two different bottles to choose from, you'd be able to make a decision much quicker and would probably be happier with your decision after the purchase.

To avoid the paradox of choice, companies will:

- Simplify their offerings
- Group similar offerings together
- Highlight recommendations

Fewer, clearer choices make customers more likely to act.

Lesson #29: Decoy Effect

The decoy effect is when companies introduce a strategically worse option to make another option look better by comparison.

The decoy is not meant to be chosen. It's there to nudge customers toward the plan, product, or option that the company really wants them to pick. It works because customers love comparing.

Example #1: A streaming service offers three plans:

- *Basic: $8/month, but with very few features*

- *Decoy: $14/month, but with fewer features than Standard*

- *Standard: $15/month*

Most people will not consider the Decoy plan because the Standard plan looks like a much better value. For just $1 more, the customer is getting much more features.

The company knows this. They included the Decoy plan to push customers towards the Standard plan instead of settling for the Basic plan.

Example #2: Imagine you're buying popcorn at the movies and see two options:

- *Small popcorn: $4*

- *Large popcorn: $7*

Let's say that you're leaning towards the small popcorn. Suddenly, a third option appears:

- *Medium popcorn: $6.75*

Now, the large popcorn looks like a great deal. It only costs 25 cents more than the medium popcorn and you get much more popcorn.

You may end up deciding to buy the large popcorn because the decoy makes it seem like better value. If the decoy wasn't there, you might have purchased the small popcorn instead.

Lesson #30: Psychological Pricing

Customers react to how prices feel, not just what they are. Prices aren't just numbers, but another way to send signals to the customer.

Here are a few psychological pricing techniques:

Charm pricing

Prices ending in 0.99 or 0.95 seem cheaper than they are. This works because customers tend to read from left to right and focus on the first digit in the price.

Example: $9.99 feels cheaper than $10.00 even though it's just one cent less.

Prestige pricing

Round numbers can signal premium or luxury.

This is often used in high-end fashion, jewelry, or premium services where perception of value matters more than affordability.

Example: $200/month feels bold, confident, and high-end compared to $199/month.

Minimal price cues

A price written in smaller font or without dollar signs can reduce the perceived magnitude of the price. This works because shorter prices look cheaper, even if they are the same amount.

Example: Instead of writing $49.00, the price can be written as just 49.

Odd vs. even pricing

Odd pricing implies a bargain or discount while even pricing implies professionalism or quality. Many businesses set their prices based on whether they want to signal value or prestige.

Example: A shirt priced at $7.47 feels like a cheap bargain. A shirt priced at $40.00 feels like higher quality.

Bundle pricing

Combining items into a single price can make them feel like a deal.

This works because customers focus on the deal instead of the per-unit cost. This also helps reduce decision fatigue by offering a simple option.

Example: A fast food combo meal for $9 feels better than paying $5 for a burger, $3 for fries, and $2 for a drink since the bundle offers savings.

Lesson #31: Default Bias

Customers tend to stick with whatever is pre-selected for them. In other words, customers tend to go with the default option, even if it's not the best.

Why?

It's easier, feels safer, and saves mental energy. This is known as default bias.

This happens because of a few reasons:

- Customers want to save time and mental energy
- Customers fear making a wrong choice
- Default options feel like recommendations

- Changing a default may feel like giving something up

Businesses can take advantage of this by setting the option they want customers to choose as the default.

Example #1: In some countries, organ donor registration is the default. Citizens need to opt-out if they wish to not have their organs donated upon death. As a result, the participation rate is nearly 100%.

In other countries, citizens have to opt-in to organ donation. Participation rates in these countries are significantly lower.

Example #2: Subscription free trials often default to auto-renew, which leads to higher conversion into paid plans. This saves the customer time, mental energy, and forces the customer to give something up if they want to cancel their subscription.

Lesson #32: Scarcity

Customers assign more value to things that are perceived as limited or rare. When something is harder to get, customers want it more.

This happens because their brains are wired to interpret scarcity as a signal of higher worth. Scarcity triggers urgency, excitement, and the fear of missing out.

Additionally, scarcity is a form of social proof. If something is scarce, that means that others want it.

Scarcity also triggers loss aversion. Customers hate the idea of missing out on a limited offer.

Example #1: A streaming service advertises: "Sign up this weekend and get 3 bonus months free. Offer ends Sunday."

The deadline pushes customers to act now. Even if they weren't planning to sign up, scarcity gets their attention and triggers an urge to not miss out on the promotion.

Example #2: Retail brands, such as Supreme or Rolex, often release limited edition items to maintain brand exclusivity and high resale value.

While scarcity increases conversions, it should be used carefully because if everything is marketed as scarce, customers may stop believing you.

5. Lessons on Companies

Overview

This section is all about companies. We'll cover the different business models that exist, how companies are measured, and how they are organized.

Here are the lessons that we'll cover:

- B2C vs. B2B
- Online vs. brick-and-mortar
- Direct vs. indirect distribution
- Marketplace models
- Licensing, franchising, and affiliate models
- Core business
- Divestiture

- KPIs and performance metrics
- Organizational structure

Lesson #33: B2C vs. B2B

When it comes to business models, one of the most common distinctions is B2C versus B2B.

B2C

B2C stands for business-to-consumer. B2C companies sell directly to consumers.

Examples of B2C companies include:

- Netflix
- Nike
- Starbucks
- McDonald's
- Spotify

The advantages of a B2C business model include:

- **Large customer base**: There are millions of potential buyers
- **Faster sales process**: Purchasing decisions are often made quickly
- **Easier to build brand loyalty**: Good design, great service, or a strong social media presence can attract and retain customers
- **Scalability**: Digital marketing can help reach millions at once

The disadvantages of a B2C business model include:

- **High competition**: There are typically many companies fighting for market share

- **Lower average order value**: One customer isn't going to spend as much as an entire business can spend

- **More emotional buying behavior**: It's harder to predict and control how customers make their purchasing decisions

- **Higher churn risk**: Customers can switch brands quickly

B2B

B2B stands for business-to-business. B2B companies sell products or services to other businesses.

Examples of B2B companies include:

- Salesforce
- Slack
- Amazon Web Services
- Oracle
- Stripe

The advantages of a B2B business model include:

- **Larger deal sizes**: One business can bring in thousands or millions of dollars

- **More predictable revenue**: Products and services are often based on contracts or subscriptions

- **Stronger client relationships**: Businesses tend to stick with vendors they trust

- **More logic-driven decisions**: There is less emotion involved in the purchasing process and more focus on return on investment

The disadvantages of a B2B business model include:

- **Longer sales process**: It can take weeks or months to close a deal

- **Smaller customer pool**: There are much fewer businesses than there are individuals

- **More complex product needs**: Businesses require more tailored solutions

- **Slower feedback loop**: It is harder to quickly test new products and offerings for businesses

Each business model has its own strategies, opportunities, and challenges.

Lesson #34: Online vs. Brick-and-Mortar

One of the biggest choices a business makes is where and how it will sell its products or services. There are two main models:

- **Online**: E-commerce or digital business

- **Brick-and-mortar**: Physical stores or locations

Some businesses stick to one model while others will do both. Understanding the advantages and disadvantages of each helps explain different cost structures, revenue strategies, and customer experiences.

Online

Online businesses sell through websites, apps, or digital platforms. Customers browse, order, and pay remotely, often from their phones or computers.

There are several benefits of an online business.

- **Lower overhead costs**: Since the business is online, there is no rent, fewer staff, and no utilities to pay

- **Scalable**: Online businesses can reach customers nationwide or worldwide

- **Open 24/7**: Customers can shop online anytime

- **Easier to track data**: Online businesses can track and analyze clicks, traffic sources, and customer behavior in real time

- **Faster to launch and test**: New products or marketing campaigns can go live quickly

The downsides of an online business include:

- **Harder to build trust**: Customers can't see or touch the product

- **High competition**: Anyone can start an online store since setup costs are fairly low

- **Shipping and logistics challenges**: Fulfillment and returns can be complex and expensive

- **Limited personal interaction**: There is no face-to-face relationship building with customers

Brick-and-mortar

Brick-and-mortar businesses sell through physical locations. Customers walk in, browse, interact with staff, and purchase in person.

There are several benefits of a brick-and-mortar business:

- **In-person experience**: Customers can see, feel, and try products

- **Stronger personal relationships**: Staff at brick-and-mortar businesses can build loyalty and answer questions

- **Impulse buying**: Customers often buy more when shopping in-store versus online

- **Easier for local brand building**: Good locations can attract regular foot traffic

The downsides of a brick-and-mortar business include:

- **Higher fixed costs**: Brick-and-mortar businesses need to pay for rent, utilities, maintenance, insurance, and staff

- **Longer setup time**: Leases, construction, and permits can take months to secure and complete

- **Geographic limits**: Brick-and-mortar businesses can only serve customers near their physical locations

- **Limited hours**: Brick-and-mortar businesses are typically closed at night or on holidays

- **Vulnerable to disruptions**: Bad weather can reduce foot traffic

Many businesses now use a hybrid model, combining online and offline to serve more customers. This model offers flexibility, but also adds complexity in managing both channels.

Lesson #35: Direct vs. Indirect Distribution

Once a company has a product, they'll need to decide how they are going to get that product to their customers. This is where distribution strategy comes in.

There are two main types of distribution:

- Direct distribution

- Indirect distribution

Each approach has its tradeoffs and businesses often choose based on factors such as cost, control, scale, and customer experience.

Direct distribution

In direct distribution, also known as direct-to-consumer or D2C, the business sells its product directly to the end customer without relying on a third party.

Example: Apple sells iPhones through its own Apple Stores and website, directly to the end customer.

The advantages of direct distribution include:

- **More control**: The company manages pricing, branding, and the full customer experience

- **Higher profit margins**: There is no middleman to take a cut

- **Faster innovation**: The company can test, learn, and make changes more quickly

- **Direct customer relationships**: It's easier to gather customer feedback and build loyalty

The disadvantages of direct distribution include:

- **Requires strong branding and marketing**: The company needs to attract customers on their own instead of relying on a third party

- **Higher initial costs**: D2C requires more upfront investment in infrastructure or technology

- **High operational complexity**: The company needs to handle everything, including logistics, shipping, and customer service

Indirect distribution

In indirect distribution, the company sells through intermediaries such as wholesalers, retailers, resellers, or third-party platforms.

The advantages of indirect distribution include:

- **Faster reach and scale**: The company can leverage existing customer networks

- **Lower upfront costs**: There is no need to build stores or infrastructure

- **Simplified operations**: Third parties handle sales, fulfillment, and customer service

The disadvantages of indirect distribution include:

- **Lower profit margins**: Intermediaries will take a cut of sales

- **Less control**: The company can't fully manage how their product is presented or priced

- **Limited customer data**: Since a middleman owns the customer relationship, the company will not be able to collect as much customer data

- **Brand dilution**: It will be more difficult for the company's products to stand out if they are sold alongside competitor products

A company might want to start with direct distribution to test the waters, then expand through indirect distribution channels to grow faster.

Other companies use a hybrid approach to take advantage of both ways of selling.

Example: Apple sells directly through its own stores and website, but also sells through retail chains and mobile carriers. This gives them both scale and control.

Lesson #36: Marketplace Models

Some of the most valuable and familiar companies in the world don't primarily sell products or services themselves. Instead, they connect buyers and sellers.

These are known as marketplace businesses.

A marketplace model is a business that acts as a platform for two or more sides of a transaction. Typically, one side provides goods and services while the other buys them.

Businesses that are a marketplace model don't own the product or service. They simply facilitate the exchange.

Examples of this include:

- **Amazon Marketplace**: Connects third-party sellers with buyers
- **Uber**: Connects riders with drivers
- **Airbnb**: Connects travelers with people renting out homes

- **Etsy**: Connects handmade goods sellers with shoppers

- **eBay**: Connects buyers and sellers in an online marketplace

These businesses typically earn money by charging a listing or subscription fee, taking a percentage of the transaction, or selling premium services or advertising.

Marketplace models are known as a two-sided or multi-sided network. To grow, the business needs to grow both the supply side and demand side at the same time.

Marketplace models benefit tremendously from network effects. The more users there are on the platform, the more valuable the platform becomes.

Example: The more drivers that are on Uber, the less riders need to wait for a driver to arrive. The more riders there are on Uber, the less drivers need to wait to be matched with a rider. So, Uber becomes more valuable as more riders and drivers join the platform.

The advantages of a marketplace model include:

- **Low initial costs**: There is no need to own inventory or hire service providers

- **High margins**: Once the platform is built, each new transaction costs very little to process

- **Strong network effects**: As more people use the platform, growth accelerates

The disadvantages of a marketplace model include:

- **Difficult to start**: The company needs buyers and sellers at the same time. Growing one side without the other is difficult

- **Control quality**: Since the company doesn't own the product or service, it's difficult to control quality

- **Trust and safety issues**: Users of the platform must trust the platform to handle payments and disputes

Lesson #37: Licensing, Franchising, and Affiliate Models

Not all businesses grow by selling directly to customers. Some expand by letting others sell their product or use their brand in exchange for a fee or share of revenue.

Three common models for doing this are:

1. Licensing
2. Franchising
3. Affiliate model

Let's take a look at each one of these models, which each have their own advantages and tradeoffs.

1. Licensing

Licensing is when a company allows another company to use its intellectual property in exchange for a fee or royalty. Intellectual property may include things such as brand name, logo, character, or product design.

Example: Disney licenses their Mickey Mouse character to toy manufacturers and clothing brands that sell toys and merchandise.

The licensor, or the company that owns the intellectual property, doesn't make or sell the product. They just give permission for another company to use it under agreed upon terms.

The advantages of licensing include:

- Earning revenue without manufacturing or selling anything yourself

- Low operational costs since licensees handle production, distribution, and sales

- Increased brand exposure without doing much work

The disadvantages of licensing include:

- Less control over how the brand is used

- Potential for brand damage if there are quality issues

- Revenue depends on another company's success

2. Franchising

Franchising is when a company allows independent operators to open and run businesses under their brand name, using their systems, products, and processes.

The independent operators are called the franchisees while the company is called the franchisor.

Typically, the franchisee pays an upfront fee and ongoing royalties in exchange for the right to operate under the brand.

Example: McDonald's is built on a franchise model. McDonald's owns the brand, business systems, and recipes. The individual franchisees pay to operate a McDonald's restaurant under that brand name.

McDonald's franchisees:

- *Pay an initial franchise fee*

- *Follow McDonald's strict standards, training, and operations*

- *Pay ongoing royalties and keep the remaining share of profits*

Businesses that use a franchise model to grow enjoy fast, low-capital expansion since franchisees invest their own money.

However, the primary challenge of a franchise model is that it's difficult to ensure high quality, good service, and consistency across all locations. One bad franchise can hurt the entire brand.

3. Affiliate model

In an affiliate model, a business rewards individuals or partners for driving traffic or sales. These individuals or partners are known as affiliates.

Affiliates send potential customers to the company, usually through unique links, codes, or partnerships, and earn money when those customers take a specific action. This may include making a purchase, signing up, or subscribing.

Example: Amazon runs the Amazon Associates program. Affiliates earn a percentage of every sale they drive.

If an Amazon Associate sends you a unique link to purchase a product and you make that purchase, they'll receive commission for the sale that they helped generate.

With an affiliate model, the company only pays when results are delivered. So, there are no upfront advertising or marketing costs.

The affiliate model is easy to scale because the company can recruit many affiliates with different audiences.

However, there are a few downsides with this model:

- The company has less control over messaging
- Affiliates may not perfectly represent the brand

- The company will need to prevent abuse when an affiliate manipulates or cheats the system to earn unfair commissions

Lesson #38: Core Business

A company's core business is the set of products or services that make up the foundation of its success. It's what drives profit, growth, and long-term stability.

Think of the core business as the heart of the company. It's the part that:

- Generates the most revenue or profit

- Has the strongest competitive advantage

- Keeps the brand relevant and trusted

Example: Nike's core business is athletic footwear. While it also sells apparel and accessories, shoes are how it got started and also its foundation.

Sometimes, companies try to grow by entering adjacent markets that are related to their core business. While this can lead to innovation, it can also backfire if they spread themselves too thin or move too far from what they do best.

Common risks of pursuing too many adjacencies include:

- **Diluted focus**: Resources get split across different things and company performance drops

- **Brand confusion**: Customers no longer understand what the company stands for

- **Poor execution**: The company lacks the expertise or infrastructure to succeed in the new area

- **Financial strain**: New ventures cost money and don't always deliver returns

A popular business strategy is to invest about 80% of resources in strengthening the core business while using the remaining 20% to explore new, related opportunities for growth.

This strategy says that the best, most sustainable growth comes from focusing on and strengthening the core business rather than constantly chasing new markets or unrelated ventures.

Lesson #39: Divestitures

A divestiture is when a company decides to sell off, shut down, or spin off part of its business. This could be a product line, business unit, brand, factory, or office location.

Divestitures are a strategic decision to focus on what matters most and get rid of what's no longer helping the company succeed.

There are many reasons why a company might choose to divest something.

- Focus more on the core business

- Get rid of a part of the business that is losing money or underperforming

- Generate cash to pay down debt, invest in growth, or return money to shareholders

- Help give that part of the business room to grow on its own

- Comply with regulations or laws that prevent monopolies

The three major types of divestitures are:

1. **Sale**: Selling the business unit to another company for cash or stock

2. **Spin-off**: Turning the business unit into a separate company and giving shares to existing shareholders

3. **Shutdown**: Closing down an unprofitable or non-core business operation

It's important to understand that divesting a part of a business isn't necessarily a sign of failure. It can be a sign of discipline and good leadership.

Successful companies routinely prune parts of the business that no longer make sense, similar to a gardener trimming branches so that the rest of the tree can grow stronger.

Lesson #40: KPIs and Performance Metrics

Businesses use metrics to track their progress and assess how they are doing. These are numbers that tell a company whether it's on track, falling behind, or outperforming expectations.

Metrics are important because if you can't measure something, it's difficult to improve it.

KPI stands for Key Performance Indicator. It is a specific and important metric that helps a business track progress toward an important goal.

KPIs vary depending on the type of business and what's being measured. A coffee shop will have very different KPIs compared to a software company.

Not every number or metric is useful. For a metric to be a good KPI, it has to be measurable, easy to understand, tied to a specific goal, and help make decisions.

Examples of KPIs include:

Revenue KPIs

- **Monthly revenue**: Total sales each month

- **Year-over-year growth**: How this year's revenue compares to last year's revenue

- **Average order value**: The average amount a customer spends per order

Profit KPIs

- **Gross profit**: How much money is left over from revenue after subtracting variable costs

- **Operating profit**: How much money is left over from revenue after subtracting operating costs

- **Net profit**: How much money is left over from revenue after subtracting all expenses, taxes, and interest

Customer KPIs

- **Churn rate**: The percentage of customers who stop buying

- **Net Promoter Score**: A measure of customer satisfaction and loyalty

- **Conversion rate**: Percentage of people who take a desired action, such as signing up or purchasing something

Operational KPIs

- **Inventory turnover**: How quickly inventory is sold and replaced

- **On-time delivery rate**: Percentage of orders delivered on schedule

- **Website traffic**: How many people visit your website

KPIs help companies stay focused and make better decisions. It can help spot problems early before they become major issues. They also ensure that everyone is aligned on working towards the same goals.

Example: A streaming service notices that churn rate is increasing. This is a red flag because it means that customers aren't finding enough value to stay subscribed to the service.

Since the company is actively tracking this KPI, they are able to identify this issue early and take action to improve customer retention.

Lesson #41: Organizational Structure

Every company needs a system for how it's organized. This includes who reports to whom, how decisions are made, and how work gets done across different teams.

That system is called the organizational structure.

A company's organizational structure defines how it arranges its people, departments, and decision-making processes to achieve its goals.

A company's organizational structure impacts:

- Speed of decision-making

- Clarity of roles and responsibilities

- Communication and collaboration across teams

The right structure helps a company move fast, stay focused, and work efficiently. The wrong structure creates confusion, bottlenecks, and missed opportunities.

There are four common types of organizational structures:

1. Functional structure
2. Divisional structure
3. Matrix structure
4. Flat structure

1. Functional structure

In a functional structure, the company is divided by department or function. Each department specializes in one area and reports to senior leadership.

Example: An electronics company may have a marketing team, finance team, product team, manufacturing team, and sales team.

This structure is simple, provides clear responsibilities, and each team has deep expertise.

However, this structure can lead to teams becoming siloed and to poor communication across departments.

2. Divisional structure

In a divisional structure, the company is organized by product line, region, or customer segment. Each division has its own mini-version of all functional departments.

Example: A fast food company might have divisions by region, such as a North America team, Europe team, and Asia team. Each region has its own marketing, finance, and operations teams.

A divisional structure allows companies to be highly responsive to local needs or specific products. There's also better accountability at the division level.

However, this structure can be expensive because of duplicate functional teams. There could also be competition or conflict across divisions.

3. Matrix structure

In a matrix structure, employees report to two managers. Typically, one is functional and one is project or product-based.

Example: A tech company may assign a marketing person to both the global marketing team and a specific product launch team.

This structure encourages collaboration across functions and is useful for project-driven organizations.

However, dual reporting can be confusing and there could be conflicts in priorities between managers. Decision-making is also slower since there are two managers to make decisions.

4. Flat structure

In a flat structure, there are few or no layers of management between employees and leadership. This is most common in startups and small companies.

Example: A startup has 18 employees that work across product, engineering, marketing, customer support, and design. All 18 employees report directly to the founder of the company.

This structure encourages fast decision-making, makes employees feel empowered, and has less bureaucracy than other organizational structures.

However, this structure can become chaotic as the company grows. There is a lack of clear career paths and leaders may become overwhelmed with so many direct reports.

Most companies don't keep the same structure forever. They adapt as the business grows, launches new products, enters new markets, or brings on more employees.

Taylor Warfield

6. Lessons on Competitive Advantage

Overview

This section is all about how companies become successful and win in the markets that they compete in. We'll look at different factors that give businesses an edge over their competition.

Here are the lessons that we'll cover:

- Competitive advantage
- Economies of scale
- Network effect
- Intellectual property

Lesson #42: Competitive Advantage

In business, the most successful companies have something that makes them stand out. They offer more value to customers or operate more efficiently than their competitors.

You may have heard of this being called having a competitive advantage.

Let's define exactly what a competitive advantage means.

A competitive advantage is a company's ability to create the biggest gap between what customers are willing to pay and what it costs the company to deliver that product or service.

The bigger the gap, not only the more profit a company can earn, but the harder it is for other players to compete.

Example: Let's say that there are two coffee shops that sell lattes.

- *Shop A uses high-end ingredients, has great ambiance, and strong branding. Customers are willing to pay $6 for their lattes and it costs the shop $2.50 to make one*

- *Shop B sells generic lattes that customers are only willing to pay $4.50 for. It costs the shop $3 to make one*

For Shop A, the gap between what customers are willing to pay and what it costs to make is $6 - $2.50 = $3.50.

For Shop B, the gap between what customers are willing to pay and what it costs to make is $4.50 - $3 = $1.50.

From these calculations, Shop A has the competitive advantage since their gap between what customers are willing to pay and what it costs the company to make a latte is the largest.

If Shop B were to drop their prices by $1.50 and make zero profit, Shop A could do the same and still make a profit of $2 per latte.

Based on our definition of competitive advantage, competitive advantage comes from:

- Increasing the customer's willingness to pay
- Decreasing costs
- Doing both

To increase the customer's willingness to pay, a company can:

- **Improve their brand and reputation**: People pay more for Starbucks coffee than generic brands because of the name

- **Offer unique features, superior quality, or specialized performance**: Apple differentiates its devices with design, ecosystem, and software integration

- **Provide an excellent customer experience**: Nordstrom is well-known for its exceptional customer service

- **Create a better design or aesthetic**: Dyson products combine performance with high-end design

- **Offer tailored or customized solutions**: Salesforce lets businesses customize their customer relationship management software to meet their specific needs

- **Use cutting-edge technology and innovation**: Tesla's autopilot and electric vehicle range were early innovation drivers

- **Make things faster or more convenient**: Amazon Prime's 2-day delivery drives customer loyalty and willingness to pay

- **Align better to customer values**: Customers buy from Patagonia because of the company's commitment to environmental sustainability

To decrease costs, a company can:

- **Achieve scale**: Walmart is a massive grocery chain that gets better deals from suppliers since they buy in bulk

- **Streamline operations and improve efficiency**: Toyota's manufacturing process cuts inefficiencies at every step

- **Vertically integrate to remove any middleman**: Netflix produces its own content to avoid licensing costs from studios

- **Choose lower cost materials or labor**: Fast fashion companies, such as Zara, use lower-cost materials and suppliers to keep costs low

- **Outsource to lower-cost regions**: Nike uses factories in Asia since they can produce more cheaply than factories in the U.S.

All of these actions help a company achieve a competitive advantage by increasing the customer's willingness to pay and decreasing costs.

Lesson #43: Economies of Scale

One source of competitive advantage that we briefly touched on is economies of scale. This is what allows large companies to offer lower prices and still make profits.

Economies of scale is the cost advantage a business gains as it produces more units of a product or service.

Example: If you're a sandwich shop that only sells 1 sandwich a month, your costs to produce that single sandwich are going to be very high.

You have fixed costs such as rent, equipment, and employee wages. You also have variable costs such as bread, produce, and meats, many of which have a minimum purchase size. It could cost $5,000 just to sell 1 sandwich.

However, let's say that you sell 1,000 sandwiches a month. Your fixed costs are now spread across 1,000 sandwiches instead of just one. More of your variable costs are going to be used instead of going to waste. It could cost as little as $5 per sandwich to produce.

Now, let's say that you sell 100,000 sandwiches a month. Your fixed costs are now spread across 100,000 sandwiches instead of 1,000.

Additionally, you can purchase bread, produce, and meats at a lower price because you have more bargaining power due to the volume that you purchase.

Now, it could cost as little as $1 per sandwich to produce.

At some point, you'll eventually reach a point where you can no longer meaningfully decrease your costs to produce one sandwich. At this point, you have reached economies of scale.

There are several things that happen as a company grows that help it achieve economies of scale:

- Fixed costs are spread over more units

- Buying in bulk gets discounts

- The cost of purchasing machinery or software that increases efficiency can be justified

- Specialization further increases efficiency and reduces costs

- Resources and infrastructure can be shared across different business units

Companies with strong economies of scale often win because they can lower prices to outcompete competitors and still be profitable.

As they gain more volume, they can further reduce their costs and lower prices even more.

This cycle repeats until the company can no longer meaningfully reduce costs, achieving scale.

However, it is possible to grow too big.

At some point, a company can reach something called diseconomies of scale, which actually raises the cost per unit. This can happen for a few reasons:

- **Bureaucracy**: More layers of management slow down decision-making

- **Communication issues**: As a company grows larger, it becomes more difficult to coordinate across teams

- **Inflexibility**: Larger companies may struggle to adapt or innovate quickly

Lesson #44: Network Effect

The network effect is a phenomenon in which a product or service becomes more valuable as more people use it. In terms of competitive advantage, it helps increase customer willingness to pay.

Example: Imagine a brand-new social media platform with only 5 users. It's not very useful because there's no one to interact with.

However, once millions of people are on the platform, it becomes way more valuable. Users can message friends and find communities. Each new user improves the experience and increases the value of the platform for everyone else.

If a new social media platform wants to compete with this one, they'll need to also have millions of people on their platform. So, the network effect helps create a barrier to entry in the market.

There are four major types of network effects:

1. Direct network effect
2. Indirect network effect
3. Data network effect
4. Standardization

Direct network effect

A direct network effect causes the value of the product or service to increase as more people of the same type join.

Example: For messaging apps, such as WhatsApp or iMessage, the more users there are, the more people there are to message. This causes more users to use the messaging app.

Indirect network effect

An indirect network effect causes the value of the product or service to increase for one group of users when a different group joins.

Example: More sellers on eBay results in more products for sale on the platform. This attracts more buyers, which then attracts even more sellers to use the platform.

Data network effect

A data network effect causes a company to gather more user data, which helps them improve their product or service, which attracts even more users.

Example: The more searches that are done on Google Search, the more data is collected, and the better the search results. Better search results lead to more users and searches, which repeats the cycle.

Standardization

In standardization, the network effect causes a product or service to be the standard in which everyone benefits from it due to compatibility.

Example: The more device makers that support USB, the more valuable it is for users because everything just plugs in and works. Eventually, USB became the standard for connecting computers and electronic devices.

Regardless of the type of network effect, companies with strong network effects enjoy:

- Stronger customer loyalty

- Faster growth through word-of-mouth

- Better user experience

- High barriers to entry for competitors

Once a network effect kicks in, it becomes a self-reinforcing loop. More users attract more users, which increases the value of the product or service, which then attracts even more users.

Network effects are one of the few advantages that actually get stronger over time.

Lesson #45: Intellectual Property

Another source of competitive advantage is having intellectual property. This refers to creations of the mind that are legally protected such that others can't use or copy them without permission.

Intellectual property can include inventions, processes, technologies, and creative works.

If a company has some kind of differentiation that causes customers to have a higher willingness to pay, they can legally protect this so that competitors can't do the same thing.

Examples of intellectual property include:

- Nike's swoosh logo
- iPhone's touch screen technology
- Pfizer's COVID-19 vaccine formula
- Dyson's design of their hair dryer

Intellectual property protection allows a company to defend its ideas or technology from competitors, allowing them to charge a premium for their unique products.

There are four main types of intellectual property that can create a competitive advantage:

1. Patents
2. Trademarks
3. Copyrights
4. Trade secrets

1. Patents

A patent is a legal right that gives the inventor exclusive control over a new invention for a limited time, typically 20 years from the date the patent was filed.

Patents are most common in industries such as pharmaceuticals, biotechnology, technology, and engineering.

A strong patent portfolio can prevent competitors from copying and can be a way to protect a company's competitive advantage.

Example: Pharmaceutical companies patent their drugs so that no other company can legally produce the same formula for many years. This gives them time to recoup their research and development costs and earn profits.

2. Trademarks

A trademark protects a brand's identity, including its logos, slogans, product names, and other symbols that distinguish it from competitors.

Trademarks help build brand recognition and trust. It helps prevent customer confusion by protecting the brand from imitators.

Example: The Nike Swoosh, McDonald's Golden Arches, and Apple's logo are all trademarked. No one else can legally use them without permission.

3. Copyrights

A copyright protects creative works, such as books, music, films, designs, and even software code.

Copyrights give the company control over how its content is used and creates an incentive to invest in original production.

Example: Netflix owns the copyright to its original content, which means no one else can distribute or sell that show without permission. This includes shows such as Squid Games, Stranger Things, and House of Cards.

4. Trade secrets

A trade secret is valuable business knowledge that's kept confidential, such as formulas, processes, or methods.

Trade secrets do not need to be filed with an organization, like a patent would. Instead, they are protected through secrecy.

Example: Coca-Cola's recipe is one of the most famous trade secrets in the world. It is not patented because a patent would eventually expire and become public. By keeping a secret, Coca-Cola can protect its formula forever.

7. Lessons on Products

Overview

This section is all about products. We'll look at the two main categories of products, how they are developed, and the typical product lifecycle.

Here are the lessons that we'll cover:

- Commoditized vs. differentiated product
- Minimum viable product
- A/B testing
- Product-market fit
- Product lifecycle

Lesson #46: Commoditized vs. Differentiated Product

One of the fundamental strategic questions that a business must answer is deciding to compete on price or on uniqueness.

This decision comes down to whether their product is commoditized or differentiated.

Commoditized products

A commodity is a product that is largely indistinguishable from other products.

Examples of commoditized products include:

- Gasoline
- Batteries
- Paper towels
- Generic prescription drugs
- Bottled water

Commoditized products tend to be standardized and easy to switch between different companies.

Customers see little or no difference between commoditized products, so price is the only thing they care about. This makes it difficult to build customer loyalty.

The only way for businesses to gain new customers is to lower their prices, which creates intense price competition.

As a result, commoditized products tend to have very low profit margins. Companies need to sell a high volume of product to generate meaningful profit.

Cost leadership is the key to winning. If you have the lowest costs, you can price your product lower than competitors and gain more customers.

Companies can also try bundling or adding on services to make their product feel less like a commodity.

Differentiated products

Differentiated products offer unique value in the eyes of the customer. This can be through design, quality, features, branding, or customer experience.

Examples of differentiated products include:

- Cars
- Skincare products
- Ice cream
- Smartphones
- Sneakers

Since customers perceive clear differences across products, they have a higher willingness to pay for certain ones. Customers also have stronger brand loyalty.

As a result, profit margins for differentiated products are significantly higher than margins for commoditized products.

Competing on value is the key to winning. Businesses have to focus on protecting or deepening the differentiation to prevent their products from becoming commoditized.

Not all products are purely commoditized or differentiated. Some start commoditized and become more differentiated over time. Differentiation can also disappear without innovations or investments in branding.

Lesson #47: Minimum Viable Product

When launching a new product or service, companies often feel pressure to make it perfect before releasing it to the public. In many cases, trying to build a perfect product from day one can be a mistake.

Instead, smart companies start with a Minimum Viable Product, also known as an MVP for short.

A Minimum Viable Product is the simplest version of a product that still delivers enough value to attract early users and gather useful feedback.

Don't think of an MVP as cutting corners. Instead, think of it as starting small, testing quickly, and learning fast.

Building an MVP helps companies:

- Launch products faster and cheaper

- Avoid wasting time on features customers don't want

- Get real-world feedback early

- Adjust and improve the product based on actual customer behavior

An MVP approach is particularly used by startups and by companies entering new markets where customer preferences aren't clear yet.

Example: When Airbnb initially launched, it didn't have a sleek app, a global network of hosts, or secure payment systems.

It started as a basic website where the founders rented out air mattresses in their own apartment to people visiting for a conference.

This small experiment proved that strangers were willing to pay to stay in someone else's home and that there was a market opportunity.

Once the founders saw demand, they improved the site, added features, and scaled the business up.

An MVP can take many forms depending on the business:

- A landing page that explains a product and collects sign-ups

- A simplified version of an app with only 1-2 core features

- A manual service that mimics what the final automated service will do

- A limited release in one market or to one type of customer

The key to an MVP is that it works well enough to test the core idea without building a full version of the product.

Lesson #48: A/B Testing

When companies want to improve a product, they don't just guess at what will improve a product, they test it. One of the most common and powerful tools for doing this is called A/B testing.

A/B testing is an experiment where you compare two versions of something to see which one performs better. This is done by showing two different versions to different people and then measuring which one works best.

Typically, customers will be split into two groups:

- Group A sees the original

- Group B sees the new version that has something about it changed

The results of the experiment are observed and analyzed to decide which version is better.

A/B testing helps companies make data-driven decisions instead of relying on opinions or gut instinct.

Example: Let's say that an online streaming service wants more people to sign up on its homepage.

- *Version A of their homepage has a red "Start Free Trial" button (original homepage)*

- *Version B of their homepage has a green "Start Free Trial" button (new homepage)*

The company randomly shows Version A to half of new visitors and Version B to the other half. After a few days, they compare results:

- *Version A: 3% of visitors sign up*

- *Version B: 5% of visitors sign up*

Based on this experiment, Version B is better. Therefore, the company makes the change to their website and can continue doing other A/B tests on their website to keep improving signups.

Another benefit of A/B testing is that it reduces risk of any changes by testing it out before fully committing. A change can be made and only shown to a small percentage of total customers before being released to all customers.

Some best practices to keep in mind for A/B testing:

- Test only one change at a time so that you know what caused the difference in results

- Use a large enough sample size because small groups can give unrepresentative or misleading results

- Run the test long enough until there is enough data to trust the results

- Continue testing and learning because A/B testing is not a one-time event

Lesson #49: Product-Market Fit

One of the biggest reasons new businesses fail is because they build a product or service that people don't really want. On the flip side, the most successful companies build something that people love and are eager to pay for.

This is the idea behind product-market fit.

Product-market fit is when a company has built a product or service that perfectly satisfies the needs of a specific market.

In other words, the product "fits" the market and there's a strong match between what people want and what the company offers.

When you have product-market fit, customers are buying, using, and recommending your product without needing to be convinced. Growth starts to happen naturally.

While you can't always measure product-market fit directly, there are strong signs when a company has found it:

- Customers are actively using or buying the product
- Word-of-mouth starts to drive growth
- People are disappointed if the product disappears
- Retention is high and churn is low
- Sales or sign-ups grow steadily with little marketing effort

You can think of product-market fit as the moment where a company stops pushing and the market starts pulling.

Without product-market fit, even the best marketing, sales team, or funding won't save a business. If a company hasn't found product-market fit, scaling the business will just accelerate failure.

Therefore, product-market fit is one of the most important milestones in business.

Lesson #50: Product Lifecycle

Every product has a lifecycle. The product is introduced, it grows, it matures, and eventually it declines.

This journey is called the product lifecycle. Understanding this can help companies make better decisions about pricing, marketing, investment, innovation, and when it might be time to phase something out.

There are four key stages in a product's lifecycle:

1. Introduction
2. Growth
3. Maturity
4. Decline

1. Introduction

In this stage, the product is brand new to the market. Sales are low, costs are high, and the company is trying to build awareness and attract early adopters.

Key traits:

- High marketing spending
- Slow customer adoption

- Operating at a loss

- Focus on proving product-market fit

Example: When smartwatches first launched, most consumers didn't know what to do with them. Companies, such as Samsung and Apple, had to spend a lot of money on marketing and education to explain their value.

2. Growth

In this stage, the product is gaining traction if it has product-market fit. More people are buying or using it, sales are accelerating, and word-of-mouth starts to spread.

This is when companies often expand, invest, and improve rapidly to build on this momentum.

Key traits:

- Fast revenue growth

- Costs start to decrease

- Profitability becomes possible

Example: After the Apple Watch was introduced and refined, interest surged. Fitness tracking, messaging, and integration with the iPhone helped it reach a wider audience.

3. Maturity

In this stage, growth slows because the product has reached most of its potential market.

Companies focus on protecting their market share, optimizing operations, and squeezing in more profit from a stable customer base.

Key traits:

- Sales start to plateau
- Competition intensifies
- Heavy focus on retention
- Focus on improving profit margins

Example: Smartwatches today are a mature product. Most tech-savvy customers already use one, so companies focus on launching improved models rather than finding new users. Improvements could include a longer battery life or additional health features.

4. Decline

In this stage, sales begin to fall. New technologies, changing customer preferences, or better alternatives start to replace the product.

The company must decide whether to reinvest, reinvent, or phase out their product or service.

Key traits:

- Declining sales
- Focus on cost-cutting
- Focus shifts to newer products
- Possibility for discontinuation

Example: When a new wearable device (e.g., smart glasses) becomes the next big thing, smartwatches will enter the decline phase.

8. Lessons on Pricing

Overview

This section is all about how companies decide to price their products and services.

Pricing is one of the most important factors that determines whether a customer will make a purchase. It is also one of the biggest drivers that impact how much profit a company makes.

Here are the lessons that we'll cover:

- Ways to price a product

- Sales cannibalization

- Transactional, subscription, and usage pricing

- Bundling

- Price discrimination

Lesson #51: Ways to Price a Product

The way a company sets its price can have a huge impact on profit, brand perception, and competitiveness.

If the price is set too high, no one will buy it. If the price is set too low, the company is leaving money on the table.

Pricing may seem simple, but it's very complex to get right.

There are three common approaches to pricing:

1. Cost-based pricing
2. Value-based pricing
3. Competition-based pricing

Let's take a look at each of these approaches in detail.

1. Cost-based pricing

This approach is the simplest and most straightforward way to price a product or service. In cost-based pricing, the company adds a markup to its cost to determine the price.

Example: Let's say it costs a coffee shop $1.50 to make a latte. If they want to make a 100% markup, they would charge $1.50 + $1.50 = $3 per latte.

This approach ensures that the company makes a profit. However, it doesn't take into account what customers are actually willing to pay or what competitors are charging.

Cost-based pricing is most commonly used in manufacturing or wholesale for low-differentiation products when costs are stable and predictable.

2. Value-based pricing

This approach sets the price based on how much value the customer places on the product. Value-based pricing typically leads to higher profit margins, especially for products that solve important problems.

Example: If a latte costs $1.50 to make, but customers believe it's premium or status-enhancing, they may be willing to pay $6 or more. This price reflects the product's perceived value, not just its costs.

Value-based pricing is most commonly used for premium or luxury products, markets where customers value design or status, and products that have few or no substitutes.

3. Competition-based pricing

This approach sets prices based on what competitors are charging. The idea is to stay in line with market prices or to deliberately undercut or premium-position the product against competitors.

Example: If most coffee shops sell lattes for $5, a new coffee shop might:

- Set their price at $4.50 to win on affordability

- Match the price of $5 to blend in

- Price at $6 to signal higher quality or exclusivity

This method doesn't consider cost or customer value directly since it focuses more about positioning in the market.

Competition-based pricing is most commonly used in competitive or commodity markets, when customers comparison-shop frequently, and when the company wants to avoid being priced out.

Overall approach

There's no one right answer to which pricing approach is best, but great pricing strategies often utilize all three approaches:

- Start with costs to make sure you cover expenses

- Understand customer value to capture as much profit as possible

- Keep an eye on competition to avoid losing market share

Lesson #52: Sales Cannibalization

Sometimes, when a company launches a new product, it not only takes sales from competitors but also takes sales from itself. This is what's called sales cannibalization.

Sales cannibalization happens when a product takes sales away from an existing product made by the same company. Instead of growing total sales, the company is just shifting purchases from one product to another.

This becomes a bad thing when:

- The new product has lower profit margins

- The new product confuses customers or weakens the brand

- Overall revenue or profit decreases

- The company has spent a lot on R&D and marketing, but doesn't gain new customers

In other words, if a new product is just replacing sales of a more profitable product, the company is worse off, even if the total units sold goes up.

Example: A streaming service introduces a cheaper, ad-supported tier. Many current, full-paying users downgrade to this tier to save money.

By introducing this new service tier, the company did not gain enough new customers to offset the decrease in revenue from many full-paying users switching to a cheaper plan.

As a result, the company is worse off and has actually decreased their overall revenue.

However, sales cannibalization is strategic and even necessary. Companies choose to cannibalize their own products in order to:

- Stay ahead of competitors

- Shift customers to higher-margin products

- Keep their brand relevant and fresh

Example: Apple regularly releases new iPhone models that cannibalize sales of older models. It is better that Apple does this than letting a competitor release a new model and take their customers.

The key is to control sales cannibalization and ensure it aligns with the company's long-term goals.

Companies can reduce harmful sales cannibalization by:

- Differentiating the new product to target a different customer segment

- Changing the price point so multiple products can coexist

- Bundling or repositioning older products for different uses

- Staggering product launches to give each product its own opportunity

Lesson #53: Transactional, Subscription, and Usage Pricing

There are many ways companies can charge customers. Three of the most common pricing models are:

1. Transactional model
2. Subscription model
3. Usage model

Each model has its own advantages and disadvantages. The one that works best depends on the product, customer behavior, and business goals.

Let's take a closer look at each to compare them.

1. Transactional model

In a transactional model, customers pay once each time they buy a product or service.

Examples:

- Buying a book on Amazon
- Booking a ride through Uber
- Paying for a haircut at a salon

Transactional models are simple to understand. Revenue comes immediately after each sale and there's no ongoing commitment from customers.

However, this model requires companies to keep bringing customers back and revenue can be less predictable or consistent.

2. Subscription model

With a subscription model, customers pay on a recurring basis, usually monthly or yearly, in exchange for ongoing access to a product or service.

Examples:

- Netflix subscription
- Gym membership
- Internet services

Subscription models provide predictable, recurring revenue. It encourages long-term customer relationships and customers typically have higher customer lifetime value.

However, this model requires strong retention to avoid cancellations or churn.

There needs to be continuous value provided to the customer to justify ongoing payment. Customers may also be more hesitant to commit to a subscription than make a one-time purchase.

3. Usage model

In a usage model, customers are charged based on how much they use the product or service. The more they use, the more they pay.

Examples:

- Utilities companies charge depending on how much water, electricity, or gas is used
- Amazon Web Services charges for how much computing power and storage is used
- Shared electric scooter companies typically charge per-minute of usage

Usage models provide flexibility for customers while attracting low commitment users.

However, it's harder to predict revenue, can be complex to communicate or track usage, and some customers may be surprised by bills if they don't manage their usage.

What pricing model is best?

The pricing model that works best depends on customer behavior, the company's sales and retention strategy, and the need for revenue predictability.

Some businesses use a hybrid approach, combining elements from multiple models.

Example: Amazon Web Services uses all three models:

- *It uses usage-based pricing and charges customers for the computing power, storage, and bandwidth that they actually use*

- *It offers subscription options for companies that want reserved capacity*

- *It offers transactional add-ons, such as purchasing support or security features*

Lesson #54: Bundling

Why sell just one product when you can sell a group of them together?

Bundling is a pricing and sales strategy where multiple products or services are packaged and sold as a single unit, often at a discount compared to buying each item separately.

Bundling can:

- Increase total revenue per customer

- Help sell less popular products
- Create a perception of value

With bundling, the whole bundle feels more valuable than the sum of its parts.

Example: Imagine that you go to a fast-food restaurant and see these prices:

- *Burger: $5*
- *Fries: $3*
- *Drink: $2*

The total if all of these were bought separately would be $10. However, the fast-food restaurant offers a combo meal with all three for $9.

The customer feels like they're getting a deal with this bundle and saving $1. Meanwhile, the restaurant is able to increase its average order size, especially if someone came in just planning to get a single burger.

There are two types of bundling:

1. Pure bundling
2. Mixed bundling

In pure bundling, customers can only buy the products as a bundle, not individually. In mixed bundling, customers can choose to buy the bundle or purchase each item separately.

While bundling sounds great, there are some risks to be aware of:

- Bundling can lead to lower profit margins if bundles are discounted too heavily
- The perceived value of the bundle may drop if customers think they're paying for things that they don't want

- There's less flexibility for customers who want only specific items

Smart bundling requires knowing what combinations customers find attractive and making sure the bundle improves overall profit, not just sales volume.

Lesson #55: Price Discrimination

Why do students get movie ticket discounts? Why are plane tickets cheaper if you book far in advance? Why do grocery stores offer coupons?

These are all examples of price discrimination, a strategy in which companies charge different prices to different customers for the same product.

Instead of setting one price for everyone, the company adjusts price to match what each type of customer is willing and able to pay.

This works because not every customer values a product the same way. Some are willing to pay more while others are only interested if there's a deal.

Price discrimination allows companies to reach more customer segments, sell more units without lowering the price for everyone, and capture higher margins from those who value the product more.

All of this has to be done carefully and legally. Different prices must be set based on clear and acceptable criteria, not on unfair or unethical discrimination.

Here are some examples of how companies use price discrimination:

Age-based discounts

Certain customer groups, such as students, seniors, or children, are charged lower prices for the same product or service. This is because these groups tend to have lower disposable income.

So, offering discounts helps attract them without losing full-price revenue from others.

Example: A movie theater charges $10 for adults and $7 for students. Although the movie is the same, students get a better deal because of their age.

Bulk discounts

Customers who buy in larger quantities pay less per unit. This encourages higher spending and rewards loyal or frequent buyers.

Example: A book store charges $15 for one book, but offers a deal: buy 5 books for $60. This brings the price down to $12 per book.

This encourages book lovers to buy more at once, increasing total transaction size. Casual book readers will continue to pay full price since they don't purchase enough books to qualify for the deal.

Coupons and promo codes

Businesses can offer temporary or selective discounts aimed at price-sensitive customers while other customers still pay full price.

Example: A grocery store sends out $1 off coupons in mailers or apps. Customers who look for savings use them while less price-sensitive customers pay regular prices.

Geographic pricing

Prices can vary by location due to differences in demand, cost of living, competition, and operational costs. This allows businesses to optimize pricing for different markets and maximize profit by region.

Example: Uber charges more in New York City than in a small town for the same distance. Higher demand and operational costs justify the price difference.

Time-based pricing

Price can fluctuate depending on when the product is purchased or used. This helps match price to customer demand over time by increasing revenue during peak times and filling capacity during slower periods.

Example: Airlines and hotels use dynamic pricing. They raise prices during holidays and weekends and offer early-bird discounts for advance bookings.

Loyalty programs

Frequent or long-time customers receive perks that effectively reduce the price of the product or service over time. This rewards retention while reducing churn and incentivizing repeat purchases.

Example: A streaming service offers 20% off the annual plan to subscribers who've been members for over a year.

9. Lessons on Operations

Overview

Operations is all of the processes, systems, and activities that a company uses to create and deliver its products or services. In other words, it's all about how work gets done.

In this section, we'll provide an overview of the common topics that come up in case interviews that focus on improving a company's operations.

Here are the lessons that we'll cover:

- Output
- Efficiency
- Process improvement
- Outsourcing
- Inventory

- Inventory turnover

Lesson #56: Output

One of the critical metrics to measure operational performance is output.

Output refers to the amount of work produced by something in a given time period. This can be a machine, person, factory, or process. The formula for output is simple:

Output = Rate * Time

This formula has various versions that apply to many different situations.

- Units Produced = Production Rate * Time

- Labor Hours = Hours Worked per Worker * Number of Workers

- Distance Traveled = Speed * Time

Example: A factory has 5 machines. Each produces 12 shirts per hour. The machines run for 6 hours per day. What is the output?

*Output = 5 * 12 * 6 = 360*

360 shirts are produced per day.

The formula for output can also be used to solve for rate or time:

- **Rate = Output ÷ Time**

- **Time = Output ÷ Rate**

Example #1: A printing press produces 200 flyers in 4 hours. What is its work rate?

Rate = 200 ÷ 4 = 50

The rate of the printing press is 50 flyers per hour.

Example #2: A bakery bakes at a rate of 150 loaves per hour. How long will it take to bake 900 loaves?

Time = 900 ÷ 150 = 6

It will take 6 hours to bake 900 loaves.

Lesson #57: Efficiency

Efficiency, also known as utilization, is a measure of how well resources are used to produce output.

It compares what a process actually produces versus what it could have produced using the same input.

Efficiency is important because it helps companies:

- Lower costs by having fewer wasted resources
- Increase output without adding more labor or equipment
- Identify bottlenecks in operations

The formula for efficiency is:

Efficiency = (Actual Output ÷ Maximum Possible Output) × 100%

Example: Suppose a customer service representative is expected to handle 50 calls a day. Yesterday, they handled 40 calls. What was their efficiency?

Efficiency = (40 ÷ 50) × 100% = 80%

The customer service representative's efficiency was 80%. This might be due to difficult customer issues or too much idle time.

Lesson #58: Process Improvement

Every business has processes that determine how products are made, how services are delivered, or how customers are helped. No process is perfect.

Process improvement is about finding ways to make those processes better. This includes finding ways to:

- Increase output
- Reduce time
- Reduce costs
- Improve quality
- Eliminate waste
- Reduce errors

Even small changes in a process can have a big impact. Common ways companies typically improve their processes include:

- Removing unnecessary steps
- Automating repetitive tasks
- Standardizing procedures so they're done the same way each time
- Rearranging the sequences of steps for better flow
- Training employees to boost speed or accuracy
- Using tools or software to speed things up

Since better processes lead to better performance, companies that constantly improve how they work are the ones that stay ahead.

Example: A coffee shop is experiencing long lines during the morning rush. After reviewing their processes, they make three changes:

1. *Move the milk and sugar station away from the pickup counter*

2. *Pre-fill cups with ice for iced drinks*

3. *Add a second employee to take orders*

As a result, customers are served faster, fewer customers walk away, and the shop increases sales during peak hours.

One of the most important things to look for in process improvement is the bottleneck.

A bottleneck is the step in a process that slows everything else down. It limits how fast the whole system can go. In other words, it's the weakest link.

Example: A sneaker factory has three steps in producing sneakers:

1. *Cutting materials*

2. *Assembling sneakers*

3. *Boxing and packaging*

If the factory can only assemble 100 pairs per hour, but cutting and packaging can handle 150 pairs per hour, then assembly is the bottleneck.

Improving any other steps won't increase total output until the bottleneck, assembly, is fixed.

Lesson #59: Outsourcing

Companies don't always do everything themselves. Sometimes, it makes more sense to let someone else handle part of the work. That's where outsourcing comes in.

Outsourcing is when a company hires an outside party to perform a task, function, or service that the company would otherwise do in-house.

Instead of building it, staffing it, or managing it internally, companies pay another company to do it for them. Outsourcing can apply to:

- Customer service
- Manufacturing
- IT support
- Marketing
- Logistics and shipping

There are several reasons why companies might choose to outsource.

- **Lower costs**: Outsourcing can reduce labor, equipment, or infrastructure expenses, especially when using providers in lower-cost countries
- **Access to expertise**: Outside providers may be more experienced or efficient at specialized tasks
- **Flexibility:** Outsourcing can scale resources up or down more easily than hiring or laying off full-time staff
- **Focus on core business**: By outsourcing certain activities or functions, a company can focus on what they do best and leave non-core tasks to others

Outsourcing isn't always the right move. There are tradeoffs to consider:

- Less control over quality and timelines

- Communication challenges across teams or time zones

- Security risks, especially with data or customer information

- Loss of in-house expertise over time

- Reputation issues if outsourcing leads to poor customer service

If not managed well, outsourcing can create more problems than it solves.

In case interviews, you might be asked to decide whether a company should outsource part of its operations. To determine this, you'll need to consider costs, quality, speed, and alignment with the company's strategy.

Another term similar to outsourcing that you should not get confused with is offshoring.

Outsourcing is when a company hires an external company, either in the same country or different country, to do a certain kind of work.

Offshoring is moving work to another country, which can be done in-house or outsourced.

Example: A U.S. clothing brand hires a California-based call center to handle customer support.

- *The call center is outside the company, so this is considered outsourced*

- *The call center is still located in the U.S., so this is not considered offshored*

The same clothing brand builds its own factory in Vietnam and hires local employees to manufacture clothing.

- *The work is done within the company, so this is not considered outsourced*

- *The work is done in another country, so this is considered offshored*

Lesson #60: Inventory

Inventory is a basic but critical part of business operations. Holding inventory helps companies meet customer demand, but managing it poorly can create serious costs.

Inventory is the stock of goods a company holds to sell or use in the production of its products or services.

There are three main types of inventories:

1. **Raw materials**: ingredients or components used to make a product

2. **Work-in-progress**: Products that are being manufactured but not finished

3. **Finished goods**: Products that are ready to be sold

Think of inventory as everything sitting on shelves, in warehouses, or in transit, waiting to be used or sold.

Example: A sneaker company might hold three different types of inventories:

1. *Raw materials such as rubber, leather, and laces*

2. *Half-assembled shoes still on the factory floor*

3. *Fully boxed sneakers in a warehouse ready for shipment*

Having the right amount of inventory is critical.

If you have too little inventory, you risk losing sales, disappointing customers, and missing out on opportunities.

If you have too much inventory, you waste money and space. If too much time goes on, your inventory may start becoming obsolete and you may have to discount them heavily or throw away unsold goods.

Inventory is a balancing act.

Inventory also isn't free. It requires money to purchase, storage space to hold, and labor to manage it. While it sits on shelves, it ties up resources that could be used elsewhere in the business.

Every dollar tied up in unsold inventory is a dollar that can't be spent on marketing, product development, or growth.

So, smart companies try to optimize inventory with different strategies, systems, and tools. Common ones include:

- Forecasting customer demand to decide how much product to produce

- Producing product only when it's needed

- Having a safety stock, which is a small buffer to avoid running out of inventory

Doing all of these things helps avoid shortages and surpluses.

Lesson #61: Inventory Turnover

Holding inventory is necessary, but holding inventory for too long can hurt a business. Companies use metrics such as inventory turnover and days of inventory to monitor this.

Inventory turnover

Inventory turnover measures how many times a company sells through and replenishes its inventory over a given period, typically one year.

This metric answers the question: how fast is the company selling what they have in stock?

Here's the formula for inventory turnover:

Inventory Turnover = Cost of Goods Sold ÷ Average Inventory

Cost of Goods Sold, also known as COGS for short, is the cost to make the products. Average inventory is the average value of inventory held over a period of time.

Example: Suppose a sneaker company has $1,000,000 in cost of goods sold for the year and an average inventory of $250,000.

Inventory Turnover = $1,000,000 ÷ $250,000 = 4

This means that the company sells and replaces its inventory four times per year.

Low inventory turnover suggests that sales may be too slow, too much inventory is sitting unsold, and money is being wasted on inventory.

High inventory turnover suggests that products are selling quickly, less money is tied up in inventory, and there is a low risk of inventory becoming obsolete.

Days of inventory

Days of inventory tells you the average number of days inventory sits before it's sold.

If you know the inventory turnover, getting the days of inventory is simple:

Days of Inventory = 365 ÷ Inventory Turnover

Example: A sneaker company has an inventory turnover of 4 for the year.

Days of Inventory = 365 ÷ 4 = 91.25

So, on average, the sneaker brand holds its inventory for 91.25 days before selling it.

High days of inventory suggests that sales may be too slow, too much inventory is sitting unsold, and money is being wasted on inventory.

Low days of inventory suggests that products are selling quickly, less money is tied up in inventory, and there is a low risk of inventory becoming obsolete.

10. Lessons on Economics

Overview

For case interviews, there are a few basic economic principles that will be helpful to know. Economics is the study of how people and businesses choose to use limited resources to satisfy unlimited wants.

It looks at how decisions are made, how markets work, and how different factors influence customer behavior.

Here are the lessons that we'll cover:

- Supply and demand

- Elastic vs. inelastic demand

- Inflation

- Interest rates

- Opportunity cost

- Imports and exports
- Economic cycle

Lesson #62: Supply and Demand

If there's one economics concept that shows up everywhere in business, it's supply and demand. This concept determines the prices you can charge, how much you can sell, and how much you need to produce.

Supply

Supply refers to how much of a product or service is available for sale. When supply goes up, there's more available in the market. When supply goes down, the product becomes scarcer.

Supply is influenced by things such as:

- Number of suppliers
- Production costs
- Availability of materials
- Technology and efficiency

Supply increases when the number of suppliers increases, production costs decrease, the availability of materials increases, and when technology improves efficiency.

Demand

Demand refers to how much people want to buy a product or service that are willing to pay for it. When demand goes up, more people want it. When demand goes down, fewer people are interested.

Demand is influenced by things such as:

- Income levels
- Consumer tastes and preferences
- The number of substitutes or alternatives
- Marketing or product awareness

Demand increases as income levels increase, the number of customers increases, the number of substitutes or alternatives decreases, and when marketing and product awareness increases.

Supply and demand together

The price of a product or service is determined by the interaction between supply and demand.

If demand increases, prices will increase since consumers are competing to get more product and are willing to pay more. If demand decreases, prices will decrease to attract more buyers since there are fewer buyers now.

If supply increases, prices will decrease since there is more availability of the product or service. If supply decreases, prices will increase since there is more scarcity.

Example: Suppose a famous artist announces a concert. There are 10,000 concert tickets available.

If 50,000 fans try to buy tickets, prices will rise. There is high demand and low supply, so some fans will still buy tickets even if prices increase.

On the other hand, if only 4,000 fans try to buy tickets, prices will drop. There is low demand and high supply. Some tickets will be unsold and prices will need to be lowered to attract more buyers.

Understanding supply and demand helps companies set smart pricing strategies, respond to market changes, and plan production and inventory.

Companies don't want to make too much of a product that no one wants. Companies also don't want to run out of product when everyone is trying to buy it.

Lesson #63: Elastic vs. Inelastic Demand

Some products fly off the shelves when prices drop. Others keep selling even when prices rise. The difference is explained by a key economics concept called the elasticity of demand.

The elasticity of demand measures how sensitive customer demand is to changes in price. If the price changes, how much does the quantity sold change?

This concept helps businesses understand how much pricing power they have over customers. It helps predict how customers will react to price changes so that they can maximize revenue and set prices strategically.

Elastic demand

A product has elastic demand when a small change in price causes a large change in quantity demanded.

Lowering the price causes demand to rise a lot while raising the price causes demand to drop sharply.

Elastic demand is common for non-essential items, products with many substitutes, and in price-sensitive markets.

Example: If a streaming service subscription raises its price from $10 to $13 a month and many customers cancel, that's elastic demand. Customers can easily switch to another streaming platform or live without it.

Other examples of products with elastic demand include:

- Movie theater tickets
- Restaurant meals
- Airline tickets
- Electronics
- Designer clothing

Inelastic demand

A product has inelastic demand when a change in price leads to little or no change in quantity demanded.

Lowering the price won't increase sales much and raising the price will still result in people buying the product.

Inelastic demand is common for necessities, products with few substitutes, and in brand-loyal markets.

Example: If the price of an asthma inhaler increases from $30 to $40, most customers will still buy it. They need it to survive and there are limited alternatives.

Other examples of products with inelastic demand include:

- Water
- Electricity
- Gasoline
- Toilet paper
- Insulin

Lesson #64: Inflation

Have you ever noticed that prices seem to increase over time? A donut that used to cost $1 now costs $3 or more. This change is driven by something called inflation.

Inflation is the rate at which the general level of prices for goods and services rises over time. It causes your money to buy less than it used to.

Historically, inflation has caused prices to increase about 3% per year. However, there are years in which inflation has been significantly higher and lower.

There are several different things that cause inflation:

- When there is too much demand and not enough supply, prices rise

- When the cost of making goods goes up, businesses pass those costs onto customers

- When wages go up, companies will raise prices to account for higher costs, which then causes workers to demand higher wages to live off of

Inflation affects everything from how consumers spend money to how businesses price their products and manage their costs.

For consumers, everyday goods become more expensive. This means that their savings loses value over time since they can buy less with it.

So, consumers may shift spending toward essentials and away from luxuries.

For businesses, the challenges of inflation include:

- Rising materials and labor costs

- Employee pressure for higher wages

- Increased difficulty planning for the future

- Decreased customer spending

Inflation is a force that every business must think about since it impacts costs, pricing, and strategy.

Lesson #65: Interest Rates

Whether you're borrowing money, saving it, or investing it, interest rates matter. It influences how people and businesses spend money.

An interest rate is the cost of borrowing money or the reward for lending it. If you borrow money, you pay interest. If you save or invest money, you earn interest.

Interest rates are typically expressed as an annual percentage.

Example #1: Suppose a company takes out a $100,000 loan at a 5% annual interest rate. At the end of the year, the company owes $5,000 in interest in addition to the original $100,000.

The 5% interest rate is the cost of borrowing money or using someone else's money.

Example #2: Suppose you put $10,000 into a savings account that earns 3% annual interest. At the end of the year, you earn $300 in interest.

The 3% interest rate is your reward for letting the bank use or borrow your money.

In most countries, a central bank sets something called the benchmark interest rate. In the U.S., that institution is the Federal Reserve.

The benchmark interest rate impacts things such as:

- Mortgages
- Credit cards
- Savings
- Bonds

For businesses, interest rates impact business loans.

Higher interest rates make loans more expensive, so fewer businesses borrow money and invest that money. Lower interest rates make borrowing cheaper, so more businesses take out loans to grow.

For consumers, interest rates also impact spending.

When interest rates are high, consumers tend to spend less and save more. When interest rates are low, consumers tend to save less and spend more.

Lesson #66: Opportunity Cost

Every business decision involves a trade-off. When you choose one option, you're also choosing not to pursue something else. This is known as the opportunity cost, the hidden price tag behind every decision.

Opportunity cost is the value of the next best alternative that you give up when you make a decision. It could be measured in dollars, time, resources, or growth potential.

Understanding opportunity cost helps businesses make smarter, more intentional decisions.

Here are some examples of opportunity costs in business:

- Using factory space to make one product means not using the space to make another product

- Spending money on marketing now means delaying product development

- Launching a new product in one region means not launching it in another region

- Hiring one candidate means passing on another candidate

Opportunity costs can be dangerous because the costs are often invisible. It's easier to see what you gained than it is to see what you missed out on.

Good business decision-making means actively thinking about:

- What else could we do with this money?

- What other use of time or people might create more value?

- Are we settling for a decent outcome when we could aim for something even better?

Lesson #67: Imports and Exports

No country makes everything it needs. Businesses buy products from abroad and also sell products to other countries.

This global exchange is called international trade and plays a big role in business strategy.

Imports

Imports are goods and services brought into a country from another country. Companies import goods in order to:

- Access cheaper raw materials and labor

- Source higher-quality components

- Gain access to specialized products or technology

- Fill supply gaps that local providers can't meet

Exports

Exports are goods and services sent out of a country to be sold abroad. Companies export goods in order to:

- Reach new customers

- Achieve economies of scale from higher production volume

- Diversify revenue beyond their home country

- Take advantage of strong demand in certain regions

Example: A smartphone company that is headquartered in South Korea might choose to import lithium batteries from China and export finished smartphones to the U.S. and Europe.

This company is using imports to reduce costs and exports to increase revenue, a common global strategy.

Risks of international trade

While international trade provides a lot of benefits, there are also some risks:

- **Currency risk**: Fluctuations in foreign currency conversions can negatively impact profit

- **Tariffs**: Taxes on imports and exports can reduce profit

- **Political instability**: Government or regulatory changes can disrupt supply chains

- **Logistical challenges**: Shipping delays or global crises can cause bottlenecks

All of the benefits of international trade should be considered alongside its risks to determine whether it makes sense for a business.

Lesson #68: Economic Cycle

The economy doesn't grow in a straight line. It moves in cycles with periods of growth followed by periods of slowdowns and recovery.

This pattern is called the economic cycle, or business cycle, and understanding it helps businesses make smarter decisions.

The economic cycle has four phases:

1. Expansion
2. Peak
3. Contraction
4. Trough

1. Expansion

The expansion phase is when the economy is growing. In the expansion phase:

- Businesses are hiring
- Consumers are spending more
- Corporate profits increase

- Wages increase

During this phase, smart businesses will invest heavily in growth by launching new products, entering new markets, building more capacity, and doing more hiring.

Businesses will raise prices carefully if demand is high but keep customer trust.

2. Peak

The peak is when economic growth is at its highest point, but is starting to slow. Inflation may start rising, interest rates may increase, and there is low unemployment.

At the peak, businesses may start to notice that costs of materials and labor are becoming expensive.

During this phase, smart businesses will try to avoid over-hiring or over-building. They may start to save money in case of a downturn.

3. Contraction

The contraction phase is the slowdown or downturn phase. In the contraction phase:

- Businesses are scaling back hiring or laying off employees
- Consumers are spending less
- Corporate profits fall
- Some businesses close or go bankrupt

In the contraction phase, a recession occurs when the economy shrinks for two consecutive quarters.

During this time, smart businesses will cut nonessential spending and try to lower their costs. They'll also focus more on their core business and less on related adjacencies.

4. Trough

The trough is the bottom of the economic cycle, when economic activity is at its lowest point. In a trough, businesses are cautious, consumer confidence is weak, but eventually things begin to recover.

Smart companies use this time to plan for a comeback. They may start testing new ideas and investing strategically.

After the trough comes the next expansion phase, which continues the economic cycle.

11. Lessons on Mergers & Acquisitions

Overview

Sometimes, instead of building or growing from scratch, a company will buy or merge with another company. This is a major growth strategy used by companies of all sizes, especially larger corporations.

In this section, we'll take a closer look at mergers and acquisitions. Here are the lessons that we'll cover:

- Mergers and acquisitions

- Post-merger integration

- Synergies

- Private equity

- Valuation

- Return on investment

- Payback period

Lesson #69: Mergers and Acquisitions

A merger is when two companies join together to form a new one.

Example: In 1999, two oil giants, Exxon and Mobil agreed to combine as equals to form ExxonMobil. This was a merger because both companies joined forces to become one new company. Both companies had similar size and power.

An acquisition is when one company buys another.

Example: In 2012, Facebook acquired Instagram for $1 billion. Instagram became part of Facebook's company but kept its brand. This was an acquisition since a larger company took over a smaller one.

Companies may pursue mergers and acquisitions for a few reasons.

- **Growth and expansion**: To enter new markets, add new products and services, acquire new customers or market share

- **Efficiency**: To cut duplicate costs, share resources, and get better deals by combining purchasing power

- **Acquire talent or technology**: To gain skilled teams or valuable intellectual property

- **Eliminate competition**: To remove a competitor from the market

There are many risks associated with a merger or acquisition.

- **Culture clash**: Different working styles, values, and leadership can cause tension between the two companies

- **Overpaying**: The acquiring company may pay too much for the target company

- **Integration issues**: Combining systems, processes, or teams can be messy and expensive

- **Regulatory challenges**: Governments may block the deal if it creates a monopoly

- **Hidden liabilities**: Acquiring a company also means taking on debt, lawsuits, or poor contracts

M&A deals are complex, expensive, and carry high risk. Even large companies often struggle to make them work smoothly.

Lesson #70: Post-Merger Integration

Buying another company is just the beginning. What comes next, the post-merger integration, determines whether the merger creates value or becomes a disaster.

Post-merger integration, or PMI, is the process of combining two companies after a merger or acquisition. PMI includes:

- Combining people and teams

- Merging technology systems

- Aligning company cultures

- Streamlining combined operations

- Delivering on promised cost savings or growth

A successful acquisition is more than just signing a deal. It's about making the two companies work together as one.

Many mergers and acquisitions look great on paper, but fall apart during execution.

Employees may feel lost or undervalued. Customers may get confused or frustrated. Leadership may be misaligned. The cultures of the two companies may not mash.

Example: Suppose a large streaming company acquires a smaller podcast app. The deal is done, but now the real work begins:

- *The streaming company needs to merge platforms so users can access podcasts and streaming content in one place*

- *Podcast employees need to understand the new organization chart and reporting lines*

- *Overlapping roles may need to be combined*

- *Customers must be informed about the changes to avoid confusion or cancellations*

- *A decision needs to be made on whether the podcast app should keep its own name or be rebranded*

Without a solid post-merger integration plan, the value that's supposed to be created from the merger or acquisition may never happen.

Therefore, PMI needs to be planned for before the deal closes. Typically, there's a dedicated integration team to ensure the merger or acquisition proceeds smoothly for everyone.

Lesson #71: Synergies

When two companies combine, the goal isn't just to be bigger, but to be better together. Ideally, the benefits that come from merging two businesses make the whole more valuable than the sum of its parts.

Synergies in business refer to the idea that two companies together are more valuable than each company alone. They are often the major reason companies do mergers or acquisitions.

If there are no synergies, the deal might not create any value.

There are two types of synergies:

- Revenue synergies
- Cost synergies

Revenue synergies

Revenue synergies happen when the combined company is able to increase sales in ways the separate companies couldn't.

Examples of revenue synergies include:

- **Cross-selling**: Selling one company's products to the other company's customers
- **Expanded distribution**: Using a larger sales force or having more physical locations
- **Stronger brand power**: Charging higher prices or attracting more customers by having a bigger brand name
- **New market entry**: Using the acquired company's local presence to enter new markets or geographies
- **Increased pricing power**: Removing competition from the market to charge higher prices

Revenue synergies are usually harder to achieve and measure than cost synergies since they depend on customer behavior.

Cost synergies

Cost synergies are savings that result from eliminating duplicate expenses or increasing efficiency.

Examples of cost synergies include:

- **Reducing overhead**: Cutting duplicate roles in HR, finance, marketing, etc.

- **Consolidating operations**: Closing redundant offices, warehouses, or factories

- **Technology integration**: Moving both companies to a single system or platform

- **Supply chain efficiencies**: Buying raw materials in larger quantities to get volume discounts

Cost synergies are often easier to identify and quicker to realize than revenue synergies. They're typically the major focus right after a deal closes.

Lesson #72: Private Equity

In case interviews, your client may be a private equity firm, so it's important that you're familiar with what these firms do and how they work.

Private equity firms buy companies, work to improve their performance, and then sell them for a profit.

It's a bit like flipping houses, but instead of renovating homes, private equity firms renovate entire companies.

Private equity firms, also known as PE firms, raise money from investors, pension funds, wealthy individuals, or endowments. They pool this money into a fund and use it to acquire businesses.

When buying a company, PE firms use a mix of investor money and debt.

The businesses that PE firms buy are usually private companies or public companies that the private equity firm takes private.

A company might agree to be bought by a PE firm because:

- The owners want a cash out

- The business needs more money to grow

- The PE firm offers expertise or connections

- The company is struggling and needs a turnaround

Not all private equity investments are complete takeovers. Some private equity investments are minority stakes where the PE firm doesn't control the company, but helps it grow.

After buying the company, the PE firm takes control to improve the company. They might do this by:

- Streamlining operations and fixing inefficiencies

- Eliminating unnecessary expenses

- Combining operations with other owned companies

- Expanding into new markets or geographies

- Launching new products or services

- Replacing executives with more experienced leaders

After a few years, the PE firm may choose to sell the company or take it public again. By this time, they hope to have generated high returns for themselves and their investors.

Example: Suppose a private equity firm buys a mid-sized U.S. shoe manufacturer.

- *They pay $300 million for the acquisition, using $100 million of investor money and $200 million in loans*

- *Over the next 5 years, they cut excess costs, streamline supply chains, and expand to new regions*

- *The company's profit grows and its value increases to $600 million*

- *The PE firm sells the company for $600 million, pays off the $200 million debt, and walks away with a big return for investors*

Lesson #73: Valuation

When you're buying a company or investing in one, you'll need to know its value. Valuation is the process of estimating the worth of a business.

Knowing a company's valuation helps answer questions such as:

- How much should we pay to acquire this company?

- What's our company worth to investors?

- Are we overpaying or getting a bargain on this deal?

There are many ways to value a business. We're not going to cover all of them, but we'll cover some of the most common methods.

Comparable company analysis

This method looks at similar companies and how much they're worth.

Example: Suppose a manufacturing company is worth 10x its annual profit. Your manufacturing company has similar profit and growth trajectory. Therefore, your company might also be worth 10x its profit.

Discounted cash flow analysis

This method estimates the value of a company based on future expected cash flows.

Example: If a pharmaceutical company is expected to generate $10M in profit in each of the next 5 years, then they could be worth up to $50M.

Precedent transactions

This method looks at how much similar companies were sold for in past merger and acquisition deals.

Example: Suppose other retail chains were acquired for 1.5 times revenue. If your retail company has $20 million in revenue, it could be worth $30 million.

Cost approach

This approach values a company by estimating the cost it would take to build the company from nothing.

Example: A software company could be worth $5 million if it takes roughly ten software engineers, that are paid $100,000 per year, five years to produce a similar software product.

Liquidation value

This method values a company by determining the cash the company would receive if it liquidated all of its assets and paid off all of its debts.

Example: If a manufacturing company were to sell all of its factory space, equipment, and intellectual property, it could get $10M. The company also has $5M in debt. Therefore, the liquidation value of the company is $5M.

Valuation is part art, part science.

There is no single correct number for a company's valuation. However, if you understand the different valuation methods and what drives value, you'll be able to make smarter investment decisions in your case interviews.

Lesson #74: Return on Investment

Return on investment, or ROI for short, measures how much profit or value you get from an investment relative to how much you spent.

Return on investment matters because it helps with decision-making. Typically, businesses want to make decisions that have the highest ROI.

ROI is also a metric that can be compared across many different things. You can compare the ROI of an acquisition, a new product launch, a new investment, a new partnership, or even a new hire.

ROI is typically measured as a percentage and can be calculated using this formula:

ROI = (Gain – Cost) / Cost

Example: Suppose your company spends $100 million acquiring a smaller competitor. As a result, the company earns an additional $25 million each year in profit over the next ten years.

ROI = ($250 million - $100 million) / $100 million = 150%

The ROI is 150%, which means that for every dollar spent, you got your dollar back and earned $1.50 in return.

While ROI is useful, remember that it doesn't take into account opportunity cost. Even if the ROI of something is positive, what else could have been done with that money to generate an even higher ROI?

Additionally, ROI doesn't take into account time. Earning a 50% ROI in one month is better than earning a 50% ROI in one year.

So, it's helpful to use return on investment alongside other metrics when making business decisions to get a complete picture.

Lesson #75: Payback Period

When making an investment, it's important to know how long it will take to get your money back from the investment. That's what the payback period tells you.

Payback period is the amount of time it takes for an investment to recoup its original cost. In other words, it is how long it takes for an investment to pay for itself.

The shorter the payback period, the lower the risk. Businesses generally prefer investments that return money sooner, especially in uncertain or fast-changing markets.

The formula for payback period is:

Payback Period = Investment Cost ÷ Annual Cash Flows

Example: Suppose your company spends $100 million acquiring a smaller competitor. As a result, the company earns an additional $25 million each year in profit over the next ten years.

Payback Period = $100 million ÷ $25 million = 4

The payback period is 4 years. In other words, the initial investment of $100 million will be completely recouped after 4 years.

Although payback period is a helpful metric, it doesn't account for profits beyond the payback point. Therefore, it's important to use this metric alongside others to get a complete picture.

Taylor Warfield

12. Lessons on Financial Statements and Terms

Overview

Financial statements are the scorecards of businesses.

They show how much a company earns, spends, owns, and owes, all in a standardized format. They're essential for understanding performance, spotting trends, and making informed decisions.

While you won't be tested on any specialized accounting or finance knowledge in your case interviews, having a basic understanding of these topics will give you a major edge over other candidates.

Here are the lessons that we'll cover:

- Depreciation
- Amortization
- Income statement

- Assets

- Liabilities

- Balance sheet

- Statement of cash flows

- Financing with debt vs. equity

- NPV

- IRR

- EBITDA

Lesson #76: Depreciation

Depreciation is the process of spreading the cost of tangible assets, such as equipment, vehicles, or buildings over their useful life. It reflects how something loses value over time due to wear and tear.

Example: Instead of recording the purchase of a $100,000 piece of equipment in the year its bought, a company spreads that cost over several years.

If the equipment is expected to last 10 years, the company might record a depreciation expense of $10,000 per year over the next ten years.

Depreciation is not a real cash expense. Businesses don't pay depreciation in cash each year. Instead, it is an accounting tool that helps businesses match expenses with revenue.

Why is this important?

If the full costs of equipment, vehicles, or buildings were recorded in the year they were bought, the company would have huge expenses that year and much smaller expenses in the following years when it doesn't make these purchases.

This would make the company's profits look inconsistent. The company would have a huge loss in the first year and large profits in the following years.

Instead, using depreciation to spread the costs over time helps provide a more accurate reporting of profit. The company's expenses are recorded in the same period as the revenues they help generate.

Example: Suppose a company has annual revenue of $200,000 and costs of $150,000. It purchases a $100,000 piece of equipment that is expected to last for 10 years.

Without using depreciation, the company would have a loss of $50,000 in its first year and a profit of $50,000 for each of the following nine years.

By depreciating the equipment over 10 years, the company would have a profit of $40,000 each year for 10 years.

There are several ways to calculate depreciation. Two of the most common methods are:

- **Straight-line depreciation**: Spreading the cost evenly over time

- **Accelerated depreciation**: Recording more depreciation in early years and less depreciation in later years

Regardless of which method is used, accounting for depreciation helps businesses see the true cost of doing business and plan better for the future.

Lesson #77: Amortization

While depreciation is used for tangible assets, amortization is used for intangible assets. This includes things such as software, patents, copyrights, and trademarks.

Amortization is the process of spreading the cost of an intangible asset over its useful life.

Example: A streaming company acquires a 10-year exclusive license for $20 million. Rather than count the $20M as an expense all at once, they amortize it over 10 years.

So, the company will record a $2M amortization expense each year for the next 10 years.

Amortization is typically calculated using a straight-line method, taking the total cost and spreading it evenly over the useful life of the asset.

Just like depreciation, amortization is not a real cash expense. Businesses don't pay amortization each year. Instead, it is an accounting tool that helps businesses match expenses with revenue when reporting profit.

Lesson #78: Income Statement

An income statement is one of the three main financial statements that public companies are required to disclose to the public.

The other required financial statements are the balance sheet and statement of cash flows. We'll get to these other financial statements in later lessons.

A company's income statement, also called a profit and loss statement, shows a company's revenues, costs, and profits over a specific period of time. Typically, it's shown quarterly or annually.

The income statement tells the story of how a company goes from revenue to profit. The typical flow looks like this:

Revenue (sales)
↓
− Cost of Goods Sold (COGS)
↓
= Gross Profit
↓
− Operating Expenses
↓
= Operating Profit (EBIT)
↓
− Interest and Taxes
↓
= Net Profit

Let's go through an example to illustrate this.

Example: A sneaker company designs, manufacturers, and sells sneakers. They have $200M in revenue. This is how much money they've earned from selling products and services to customers.

Their COGS is $80M. This is the cost of manufacturing those sneakers, which includes the costs of raw materials and labor.

This leaves $120M in gross profit.

The company has $70M in operating expenses. This includes costs for marketing, rent, research and development, depreciation of equipment, and amortization of patents.

This leaves $50M in operating profit.

The company pays a total of $15M in interest on their loans and in taxes to the government.

This leaves $35M in net profit.

Lesson #79: Assets

Assets are resources a company owns or controls that provide value and help the company generate future profits. In other words, assets are things the company has that are worth something.

Examples of assets include:

- Cash
- Inventory
- Property
- Equipment
- Buildings
- Vehicles
- Patents
- Trademarks
- Brand names

Assets are crucial because they enable the company to produce and sell products and services. They also represent the company's investment in future growth.

Lesson #80: Liabilities

If assets are what a company owns, liabilities are what a company owes.

Liabilities are a company's financial obligations to others. These can be to lenders, suppliers, employees, customers, or the government.

Examples of liabilities include:

- Money owed to suppliers

- Salaries owed to employees

- Taxes that need to be paid

- Business loans

- Leases

- Pension obligations

Liabilities are not always bad.

Debt, for example, can help companies grow as long as they can manage it wisely. However, having too many liabilities can create risk, slow growth, or lead to bankruptcy.

A healthy income statement should show consistent revenue growth, healthy gross margin, controlled operating expenses, and a positive net profit.

Lesson #81: Balance Sheet

The balance sheet is the second major financial statement that all public companies are required to disclose to the public.

Unlike the income statement, which shows how a company is performing over time, the balance sheet tells you where a company stands at a specific moment in time.

The balance sheet shows everything the company owns, owes, and what's left over for owners. There are three major components of a balance sheet:

1. **Assets**: What the company owns

2. **Liabilities**: What the company owes

3. **Equity**: What's left for the owners after subtracting liabilities from assets

Let's take a look at an example of a balance sheet.

Example: Suppose you're looking at the end of year balance for a sneaker manufacturer.

Assets: $50M

- *Cash: $10 million*

- *Inventory: $15 million*

- *Equipment and factories: $25 million*

Liabilities: $20M

- *Amount owed to suppliers: $8M*

- *Long-term loan: $12M*

Equity: $30M

This balance sheet shows that the company owns $50M in assets, owes $20M to others, and the remaining $30M belongs to shareholders or owners of the company.

In addition to the income statement, the balance sheet is helpful for understanding if a company is doing well financially. A healthy balance sheet should show strong assets, low to manageable debt, and a balance between growth and stability.

Lesson #82: Statement of Cash Flows

A business can be profitable, but still run out of cash. That's why the statement of cash flow exists. It tracks the actual movement of cash into and out of a company.

The statement of cash flows is the third and final major financial statement that all public companies are required to disclose to the public.

The statement of cash flows is broken into three sections:

1. Operating activities
2. Investing activities
3. Financing activities

1. Operating activities

The operating activities section shows cash generated or used by the day-to-day business. It includes:

- Cash from customer payments
- Cash paid to suppliers
- Cash paid to employees
- Interest payments
- Tax payments

2. Investing activities

The investing activities section shows cash spent or received from long-term assets. It includes:

- Buying and selling of equipment
- Buying and selling of factories
- Buying and selling of property

3. Financing activities

The financing activities section shows cash exchanged with investors and lenders. It includes:

- Borrowing or repaying loans
- Issuing or buying back stock
- Paying dividends.

Example: Suppose a sneaker company has the following statement of cash flows:

- *Cash from operations: +$45M*
- *Cash from investing: -$20M*
- *Cash from financing: -$10M*

This shows that the company's core business of selling sneakers generated $45 million in cash. The company invested $20M in things such as new factory equipment. It also may have paid off $10M in debt.

Overall, the company's cash went up by $15M for the year.

The statement of cash flows is useful for understanding how a company is funding its operations or growth. It helps identify companies that are profitable on paper, but struggling in real life.

Lesson #83: Financing with Debt vs. Equity

When a company needs money to grow, it has two options. It can borrow money or it can sell ownership in the company.

Both options can help the business build a new factory, launch a new product, or expand internationally, but they come with different trade-offs.

Debt financing

Debt financing is when a company borrows money from a lender, such as a bank or bondholder, and promises to pay the money back with interest.

This is similar to taking out a mortgage or student loan. You get money now and you agree to pay it back later with regular payments.

The biggest advantage of debt financing is that you get to keep ownership of the company. Once the debt is paid back, there's no further long-term obligation.

Interest is also tax deductible. This means that it helps reduce the amount of taxes a company has to pay on its profits.

A downside of debt financing is that missed payments can lead to penalties or bankruptcy. Too much debt is risky, especially if cash flow is unstable.

Newer or riskier companies may also have higher interest rates, which can make borrowing money expensive.

Equity financing

Equity financing is when a company raises money by selling shares of ownership to investors. This could involve bringing in venture capital, private investors, or going public and listing shares on the stock market.

The biggest advantage of equity financing is that no repayment is required. Companies are not obligated to pay investors back like a loan.

This can be helpful for startups that don't have stable cash flow.

The largest downside of equity financing is that you give up ownership. Investors now own part of the company. These investors may want decision-making power, which means less control over the company.

The best option for financing depends on cash flow stability, risk appetite, growth potential, and desire for control. Most companies use a mix of both debt financing and equity financing to raise money for growth.

Lesson #84: Net Present Value

Net present value, or NPV for short, measures how much an investment is worth today based on its expected future cash flows. It tells you whether the future money you'll make from an investment is worth more than the money you're putting in today.

If NPV is positive, the investment adds value. If NPV is negative, the investment loses value.

The idea behind net present value is that a dollar today is worth more than a dollar tomorrow because you can invest it, earn interest, or use it immediately.

This is called the time value of money.

NPV adjusts future cash flows to reflect this by discounting them to their present value. This is the basic formula for NPV:

NPV = Present Value of Future Cash Flows – Initial Investment

To calculate the present value, you use a discount rate, which reflects the opportunity cost of the investment.

Example: Suppose a sneaker company wants to invest $10M to build a new factory. It expects to earn the following additional cash flows over the next 3 years:

- Year 1: $4 million
- Year 2: $4 million
- Year 3: $4 million

Let's say that the discount rate for the company is 10%. This is based on the opportunity cost of building a factory. If the company were to use the $10M to invest in something else, they'd expect a 10% return on investment each year.

We can use a calculator or spreadsheet to calculate the present value of the future cash flows.

- Year 1: $4 million $\div 1.1 \approx$ $3.64 million
- Year 2: $4 million $\div 1.1^2 \approx$ $3.31 million
- Year 3: $4 million $\div 1.1^3 \approx$ $3.01 million

Notice that in year 1, we divide by the discount rate once. In year 2, we divide by the discount rate twice. In year 3, we divide by the discount rate three times.

This is because the discount rate, or opportunity cost, reflects the annual time value of money. Each year into the future, money is worth less and less.

NPV $\approx$ $3.64 million + $3.31 million + $3.01 million - $10 million

NPV $\approx$ -$40,000

The NPV is slightly negative, which means the investment would not generate a return that is greater than the company's opportunity cost. Therefore, the company should not invest in the new factory.

Notice that even though the future cash flows total $12 million, which is greater than the $10 million investment, NPV reveals that this is not a good investment because of the opportunity cost.

Although you won't be expected to do any NPV calculations in a case interview, it's helpful to understand what NPV is conceptually.

Lesson #85: Internal Rate of Return

Internal rate of return, or IRR for short, is a cousin of the Net Present Value. However, instead of telling you the value created in dollars, it tells you the return as a percentage.

IRR is the annual percentage rate at which the present value of a project's future cash flows equals its initial investment. In other words, it's the discount rate that makes the NPV = 0.

Companies often use IRR to compare investment opportunities, especially when deciding between two or more projects.

If IRR is greater than the company's discount rate, the investment adds value. If IRR is less than the company's discount rate, the investment loses value.

Remember, a company's discount rate is the company's opportunity cost. It is the return the company expects from an alternative investment.

Example: Suppose a sneaker company wants to invest $10M to build a new factory. It expects to earn the following additional cash flows over the next 3 years:

- *Year 1: $4 million*
- *Year 2: $4 million*
- *Year 3: $4 million*

Let's say that the discount rate for the company is 10%. This is based on the opportunity cost of building a factory. If the company were to use the $10M to invest in something else, they'd expect a 10% return on investment each year.

An IRR calculator or spreadsheet will calculate the IRR of the investment as roughly 9.9%. This means that the factory investment is expected to return about 9.9% per year over its lifetime.

Since the sneaker company could have gotten a 10% return through other investments, this project is not worth pursuing.

In a case interview, you won't be asked to calculate IRR since it requires software or a spreadsheet. However, you should understand what it means and how it's used to assess investment opportunities.

Lesson #86: EBITDA

EBITDA is the last financial metric that you should be familiar with. It occasionally makes an appearance in case interviews.

EBITDA stands for Earnings Before Interest, Taxes, Depreciation, and Amortization.

While EBITDA doesn't show up in any of the major financial statements, it is still widely used because it assesses a company's performance without being affected by financing decisions or accounting methods.

Example: Imagine two different lemonade stands:

- Both make $1,000 in sales each month

- One owns a fancy lemon juicer that depreciates at $10 per year while the other rents equipment

- One is in a high-tax area while the other is in a tax-free area

- One took out a large loan while the other didn't

Even though the two lemonade stands have very different net profits, their EBITDA could be the same.

This means that the two lemonade stands' core business of making and selling lemonade performed equally well. However, their net profits are impacted by the different financial decisions that were made and their different tax situations.

EBITDA is also used in determining the valuation of a company. Many companies are valued using a multiple of EBITDA.

Example: A company has an EBITDA of $1M. Similarly sized companies in their industry have been acquired for 10x EBITDA.

Based on this, the company's valuation could be around $10M.

EBITDA can be calculated in two different ways:

1. **EBITDA = Revenue – Operating Expenses (excluding depreciation and amortization)**

2. **EBITDA = Net Profit + Interest + Taxes + Depreciation + Amortization**

Example: A company has:

- *Revenue: $200M*

- *Operating expenses (excl. depreciation and amortization): $120M*

- *Depreciation: $15M*

- *Amortization: $5M*

- *Interest: $10M*

- *Taxes: $30M*

- *Net profit: $20M*

EBITDA = $200M - $120M = $80M

This can also be calculated by starting with net profit and adding in interest, taxes, depreciation, and amortization.

EBITDA = $20M + $10M + $30M + $15M + $5M = $80M

13. Lessons on Different Industries

Overview

While most consulting firms don't expect you to have any prior industry knowledge in your case interviews, understanding the basics of how each industry works can give you a significant advantage.

In this section, we'll give you a basic primer on the most common industries that show up in case interviews.

Here are the industries that we'll cover:

- Healthcare

- Technology

- Media and entertainment

- Telecommunications

- Financial services

- Manufacturing
- Retail
- Utilities and energy
- Materials and industrials
- Hospitality and travel
- Transportation and logistics
- Real estate
- Government
- Non-profit

Lesson #87: Healthcare Industry

The healthcare industry is massive, complex, and one of the most commonly used industries in case interviews.

To succeed in a healthcare case, you don't need to be a doctor, but you do need to understand the basics of who the players are, how money flows, and how care is delivered and paid for.

Key players

The two key players in the healthcare industry are providers and payers.

Providers are the people and organizations that deliver care. They include:

- Hospitals
- Clinics

- Urgent care centers
- Pharmacies
- Imaging and lab services
- Nursing homes
- Rehabilitation centers

Payers are the entities that pay for care. They include:

- Private insurance companies
- Government
- Employers who fund employee plans
- Patients themselves

How providers get paid

There are three main ways that providers are paid for the care that they deliver. These models shape how providers behave.

1. **Fee-for-service**: The provider gets paid for each individual service delivered (e.g., a test, surgery, or office visit)

2. **Capitation / per member per month**: The provider is paid a fixed amount per patient per month, regardless of how many services that patient uses

3. **Value-based care**: Providers are paid based on patient outcomes and quality of care

There is no single best model since each has their own unique disadvantages.

Fee-for-service may lead to providers performing unnecessary procedures since they earn more money by doing more services.

Capitation may lead to under-treatment if providers are trying to keep costs low.

Value-based care sounds good in theory, but can be expensive and difficult to implement and measure patient outcomes.

Characteristics of the healthcare industry

Here are a few additional things that you should know about the healthcare industry:

- **Highly regulated**: The FDA (Food and Drug Administration) approves drugs and medical devices while the CMS (Centers for Medicare & Medicaid Services) set pricing and reimbursement standards

- **Ethical considerations**: The decisions in the healthcare industry impact lives, not just profits

- **Slow innovation**: Drugs can take 10+ years to develop and cost $1B+ to develop

- **Highly fragmented**: There are many different players in the healthcare system and each player has different incentives

- **High fixed costs**: Many healthcare businesses, especially hospitals, have high fixed costs, which means patient volume needs to be high to be profitable

- **Consolidation trends**: Hospitals, physician practices, and insurers are consolidating with some payers also becoming providers

Lesson #88: Technology Industry

The technology industry is one of the fastest growing sectors in the world. From smartphones to artificial intelligence, technology powers how people work, communicate, and live.

This industry includes companies that create, sell, or enable technology-based products or services. These can be physical or digital products.

Tech companies use a variety of different revenue models. Here are the most common ones:

Hardware sales

In this model, revenue comes from selling physical devices. This model is most common for hardware products, such as smartphones, laptops, and servers.

Margins for these products can be high, but companies face:

- **Inventory costs**: Companies must manage unsold stock, which ties up capital and risks becoming obsolete as technology improves

- **Supply chain risks**: Hardware products typically source components from many suppliers requiring complex coordination and vendor dependency for components that only have a few suppliers

- **Fast product cycles and innovation pressure**: Technology evolves quickly and companies must constantly innovate to stay competitive

Software subscriptions (SaaS)

In this model, customers pay a monthly or yearly fee to use software, which is typically delivered over the internet. This is called SaaS or software-as-a-service.

This revenue model provides many benefits:

- **Recurring revenue**: Subscriptions make revenue very predictable since customers pay every year

- **High gross margins**: Software has low costs once its developed. So, most of the revenue is profit after initial development

- **Ease of scaling**: New customers can be added with minimal cost since software can be distributed instantly online

However, it also comes with challenges:

- **Churn risk**: Customers can cancel at any time. Customer retention is critical

- **High competition**: Many software markets are crowded, forcing companies to differentiate on features, price, or user experience

- **Infrastructure dependency**: Outages, bugs, or poor performance can damage customer trust and lead to cancellations

Additionally, many companies offer a tiered pricing model. The more features that are included in the product, the higher the subscription price.

Some companies even offer the basic version of the product for free and will try get customers to upgrade to a more premium version with more features. This is known as a freemium model.

Advertising

In this model, companies monetize through ads while providing a free-to-use platform. Examples include Google, Facebook (Meta), TikTok, and YouTube.

Revenue depends on a few factors:

- **Size and engagement of the user base**: More users and longer time spent on the platform lead to more ads shown

- **Ad targeting capabilities**: Better data and algorithms allow more relevant ads, which advertisers are willing to pay more for

- **Advertiser demand**: Revenue grows when businesses see value in advertising on the platform

Online marketplaces

In this model, companies provide a platform to connect buyers and sellers. In exchange, they take a cut of each transaction that happens on the platform.

Examples include Uber, Airbnb, and Etsy.

This model relies heavily on:

- **Network effects**: The more users on the platform, the more valuable it becomes to both buyers and sellers

- **Platform trust and usability**: Users must feel safe and find the platform easy to use or they'll go elsewhere

- **High volume of transactions**: Marketplaces typically operate on thin margins. So, profitability depends on scale

Lesson #89: Media Industry

The media industry is all about creating, distributing, and monetizing content. This includes news, music, video, podcasts, and social media.

Unlike other industries, the key focus of media is on audience attention and engagement.

Common revenue models

Advertising

Many media companies offer free content and monetize by selling ad space in the content. The revenue generated depends on audience size, viewer engagement, and ad targeting capabilities.

Subscriptions

Many companies use a subscription model in which users pay a recurring fee to access content. Revenue is recurring and more predictable, but depends heavily on retaining users.

Licensing

Companies can sell or license their content to other platforms for redistribution.

Pay-per-view

In this model, customers pay for individual pieces of content.

Merchandising and experiences

Successful content can lead to branded merchandise, live events, and unique experiences.

Common industry challenges

- **Content saturation**: There's an overwhelming amount of content available, making it difficult for media companies to stand out or retain attention

- **Subscription fatigue**: With so many platforms charging monthly fees, customers are getting more selective about which services they keep, leading to higher churn and tougher competition

- **Changing consumer preferences**: Customers constantly shift toward new content and formats, requiring media companies to adapt quickly or risk becoming irrelevant

- **Platform dependence**: Media brands rely heavily on platforms such as Facebook (Meta), Google, or YouTube for distribution. A change in platform algorithms or policies can significantly affect traffic and revenue

- **Piracy and copyright enforcement**: Digital content is easy to copy and share illegally, reducing potential revenue

Lesson #90: Telecommunications Industry

The telecommunications industry, or telecom industry for short, provides the infrastructure and services that allow people and businesses to communicate over distances.

This includes wireless and mobile services, landline services, broadband internet, satellite, and cable.

Key drivers of success

Network quality and coverage

A telecom provider's competitive edge depends on how extensive, fast, and reliable their network is

Innovation and technology upgrades

Staying current with new technologies (e.g., 5G, fiber optics, Internet of Things capabilities) helps companies retain and grow market share.

Efficient capital investments

Building and maintaining telecom infrastructure is expensive. Companies that allocate their resources strategically can improve profit margins.

Customer retention

With intense competition and commoditized services, keeping customers loyal is critical. Great customer service, customer loyalty programs, and bundling can help reduce churn.

Common industry challenges

- **High infrastructure costs**: Building and maintaining networks requires billions of dollars, creating a huge barrier to entry for new players

- **Price competition**: Many telecom services have become commoditized, leading to price wars that decrease profit margins

- **Regulatory pressures**: Telecom companies are heavily regulated. Rules around pricing, data privacy, and competition can greatly impact profitability

- **Technology shifts**: Rapid technological changes require constant investment. Missing a new tech wave can lead to losing significant market share

Lesson #91: Financial Services Industry

The financial services industry is the backbone of the economy. It includes companies and institutions that manage money, facilitate transactions, provide credit, and help individuals and businesses grow wealth.

Due to the risk of financial collapse or consumer harm, financial services are tightly regulated by the government.

The financial services industry is also built on trust. If customers lose confidence, firms can collapse quickly.

Let's take a look at the major segments of this industry.

Banking

Banks serve individuals and businesses. They provide:

- Checking and savings accounts
- Personal loans
- Mortgages
- Auto loans
- Credit cards
- Business loans

Banks typically make money by lending out deposits at higher rates than they pay customers.

Example: A bank may pay you 1% interest on your savings, but they will charge 6% interest on a mortgage.

Asset and wealth management

Asset and wealth management firms invest money on behalf of individuals or institutions.

Asset management typically focuses on managing and growing a portfolio to maximize investment returns, taking into account the client's risk tolerance and goals.

Wealth management takes a more holistic approach to managing a client's overall financials, including managing investments and also helping with financial planning.

These firms earn fees based on how many dollars they are managing, also known as assets under management.

Example: An asset management firm manages $100M and charges a 1% management fee each year. Based on this, they'll make $1M a year based on their current assets under management.

Insurance

Insurance companies collect premiums from customers and pay out claims when things go wrong.

Premiums are what customers pay each month to keep their insurance coverage. They are like a subscription fee for protection.

Claims are formal requests customers make to the insurance company asking for payment or coverage after a loss, damage, or other event covered by their insurance policy.

Common insurance products include:

- Life insurance

- Health insurance

- Auto and home insurance

- Commercial insurance for businesses

Insurance companies make money by charging more in premiums than they pay out in claims. They also will invest the money they hold between collecting premiums and paying claims.

Payment processors

Companies such as Visa and Mastercard don't lend or hold money, but facilitate transactions between buyers and sellers.

They make money by charging a small percentage of each transaction.

Fintech

Fintech is short for financial technology. Fintech companies use software to disrupt traditional financial services.

Examples of fintech services include:

- Peer-to-peer lending
- Robo-advisors
- Mobile payments
- Digital banks

Fintech companies focus on lowering fees for customers, improving user experience, and reaching underserved markets.

These companies can make money in a variety of different ways, such as charging for subscriptions, transaction fees, or monetizing customer data.

Lesson #92: Manufacturing Industry

Manufacturing is the process of taking raw materials and transforming them into finished products that people want to buy. The manufacturing industry includes everything from massive car factories to small workshops making custom furniture.

How manufacturing companies make money

Manufacturing companies generate revenue by selling products for more than it costs to make them. This sounds simple, but the path to profitability involves several key factors:

- **Volume**: Most manufacturing operations have high fixed costs. Therefore, manufacturers need to produce large quantities to spread these costs across many products and achieve profitability

- **Efficiency**: Small improvements in production speed, waste reduction, or quality can translate to millions in savings when multiplied across thousands or millions of products

- **Timing**: Manufacturing companies must predict what customers will want months or years in advance since it takes time to set up production lines and build inventory

These are the major cost components of manufacturing companies:

- **Materials**: Raw inputs used to produce goods

- **Labor**: Includes assembly workers, engineers, quality inspectors, and managers

- **Equipment and facilities**: Includes machinery, tools, factories, and maintenance

- **Overhead**: These are indirect costs such as utilities, insurance, safety compliance, and administrative support

Manufacturing fulfillment strategies

There are three main manufacturing fulfillment strategies. These strategies are how a manufacturing business decides to time production relative to customer demand.

1. Make to Stock (MTS)

With this fulfillment strategy, products are manufactured in advance based on demand forecasts and are stored in inventory until sold. This is most commonly used for products that are standardized and have predictable demand.

Make to Stock ensures fast delivery to customers, but there is a risk of overproduction or obsolete inventory if forecasts are wrong.

2. Make to Order (MTO)

With this fulfillment strategy, production begins only after a customer places an order. Nothing is made in advance. This is most commonly used for products that are highly customized or have low volume.

Make to Order has low inventory risk, but longer delivery times and can be harder to scale up as demand increases.

3. Assemble to Order (ATO)

Assemble to Order is a mix of Make to Stock and Make to Order.

With this fulfillment strategy, key components are produced and stocked in advance, but final assembly happens after the customer order is received.

This is most commonly used for products that have many different configurable options.

The advantage of this fulfillment strategy is that it is faster than Make to Order and more flexible than Make to Stock. However, it requires accurate forecasting of components and more complex inventory management.

Common industry challenges

Manufacturing companies face several common challenges. These frequently appear in case interviews:

- **Capacity utilization**: Ensuring factories are producing close to their full potential without excessive downtime or bottlenecks. Low utilization can lead to higher per-unit costs

- **Quality control**: Maintaining consistent product quality while minimizing defects, rework, and waste. Poor quality can hurt reputation and increase costs

- **Supply chain disruptions**: Delays or shortages in raw materials due to supplier issues, geopolitical events, or logistics breakdowns. These can halt production

- **Technology transitions**: Updating or replacing legacy equipment and systems with newer technology. This can improve efficiency but requires upfront investment and retraining workers

Lesson #93: Retail Industry

Retail refers to the sale of goods or services directly to consumers, typically in small quantities.

Retailers are the last step in a supply chain, they buy products from manufacturers or wholesalers and then sell them to end customers.

Here are the key components of the retail business model:

Inventory

Retailers buy products upfront, hold them as inventory, and then sell them to customers. The difference between what they pay for the product and what they sell it for is their gross margin.

They must carefully balance having enough product to meet demand and avoiding too much inventory that ties up cash or becomes outdated.

Retailers rely on an efficient supply chain to stay competitive. This includes sourcing from suppliers and managing shipping and logistics. Delays or disruptions can significantly hurt profits.

Sales channels

Retailers may operate in physical stores or online storefronts. There is a trend of moving towards omnichannel, a seamless mix of brick-and-mortar and e-commerce.

Example: A customer can order a product online and pick it up in store.

Shelf space

For brick-and-mortar stores, shelf space is important because most purchasing decisions happen at the point of sale.

When customers walk down an aisle, products with more prominent placement and greater shelf presence have higher chances of being noticed, considered, and purchased.

Just as businesses will pay more for a storefront on a busy street corner, companies compete intensely for the most visible and accessible shelf positions.

Customer experience

In retail, the customer experience is everything. Retailers heavily invest in:

- Store design
- Website usability
- Checkout convenience
- Returns and customer service
- Customer loyalty programs

Strong brands create emotional connections with customers that drive repeat purchases.

Pricing strategy

Retail pricing is complex and competitive. Retailers use a mix of different pricing strategies:

- **Everyday low pricing**: Set the lowest price for certain products to attract customers

- **High-low pricing**: Set prices high and then run promotions or discounts to make the customer feel like they are getting a great deal

- **Dynamic pricing**: Adjusting price based on demand, time, or competition

Profit margins in the retail industry are thin. So, pricing decisions have a huge impact.

Seasonality

Retail sales often vary by season, including back-to-school, holidays, and by weather.

Sales are generally not consistent throughout the entire year. The busiest months for sales are typically October to December while the slowest months are January and February.

Therefore, retailers must forecast demand accurately and plan inventory accordingly.

Lesson #94: Utilities and Energy Industry

The utilities and energy industry powers almost everything, from lighting homes to fueling vehicles to powering cloud servers.

Utilities

Utilities companies provide essential services such as electricity, water, natural gas, and sewage.

In many regions, these companies have monopolies or near-monopolies due to the high upfront costs of building the necessary infrastructure.

It's generally more efficient for a single utilities company to provide services to a region rather than multiple companies duplicating infrastructure like power lines or water pipes.

While utilities companies have monopolies, they are heavily regulated by government bodies to protect consumers from potential abuses of this power. Regulation ensures fair pricing and reliable service.

Utilities companies often operate under a cost-plus pricing model in which they charge customers a rate that covers their costs and guarantees a rate of return.

Some regions also charge more during peak hours, typically the evening.

Energy

The broader energy industry includes:

- Fossil fuels (e.g., oil, natural gas)

- Renewable energy (e.g., solar, wind, hydropower, geothermal)

There are three stages in the oil and gas supply chain:

1. **Upstream**: This sector focuses on finding and extracting oil and gas

2. **Midstream**: This sector connects upstream and downstream operations and involves the transportation and storage of crude oil and natural gas before they are refined

3. **Downstream**: This sector focuses on processing and distributing the refined products to consumers

A major trend is the shift from fossil fuels to renewable energy. Governments often offer subsidies or tax credits to accelerate this transition.

Energy is also deeply tied to geopolitics.

Oil prices are influenced by wars and global supply and demand. Countries typically want energy security to reduce reliance on imported fuels. So, this results in a push for domestic production and tariffs or subsidies to protect national energy interests.

Lesson #95: Materials and Industrials Industry

The materials and industrials industry is the backbone of all physical goods that are made. These companies are responsible for producing raw materials, machinery, and infrastructure needed by nearly every other industry.

Materials

The materials sector includes companies that extract or process raw materials such as:

- Metals (e.g., steel, copper, aluminum)

- Chemicals

- Construction materials (e.g., cement, glass)

- Paper, packaging, and forestry products

These businesses often operate in commodity markets, meaning that prices are driven by global supply and demand rather than by brand loyalty or product differentiation.

Products from different suppliers are largely interchangeable. So, companies have little control over pricing.

The materials sector is also highly cyclical. Demand for materials rises and falls with the economic cycle.

Industrials

The industrials sector produces goods used in construction, transportation, and manufacturing. Examples include:

- Construction equipment (e.g., bulldozers, cranes, excavators)

- Aerospace and defense (e.g., aircraft, fighter jets, missiles)

- Industrial machinery (E.g., engines, factory automation systems, turbines)

Sales may be project-based and irregular, which causes inconsistent revenue and dependency on a few large contracts. So, industrials companies often rely on large B2B contracts and long-term government or corporate spending budgets.

Many industrials companies also make money on spare parts, service contracts, and upgrades or retrofits. These can be a source of ongoing revenue compared to one-time sales of equipment.

Common industry challenges

Here are some common industry challenges that you should be aware of:

- **High capital intensity**: High investment is required in plants, machinery, and other infrastructure

- **Increasing vertical integration**: Many companies control multiple steps in the supply chain to help manage costs, reduce risks, and control quality

- **Scale is necessary**: Profit margins are thin. So, large-scale production is necessary to lower the average cost per unit

- **Capacity management**: Building new capacity takes years and is expensive, requiring companies to balance having too little capacity and too much

- **Commodity price fluctuations**: Profitability can change dramatically when raw material prices change

- **Technical expertise**: Companies that can solve complex engineering problems or improve product performance often command higher prices and customer loyalty. This is the only way to achieve some level of differentiation

- **Environmental regulations**: This industry is one of the most scrutinized in terms of environmental impact, especially for mining, chemicals, and construction

Lesson #96: Hospitality and Travel Industry

The hospitality and travel industry is all about helping people feel comfortable and enjoy experiences away from home. This industry sells services and experiences, not physical products.

Companies in this industry include:

- Hotels
- Airlines
- Cruise lines
- Theme parks
- Casinos
- Restaurants

Key drivers for success

There are a number of drivers that greatly impact a company's success in the hospitality and travel industry.

Occupancy and capacity

Whether it's hotel rooms, airplane seats, cruise cabins, or restaurant tables, maximizing usage of existing space is crucial. The more rooms or seats filled, the more efficiently the business spreads its costs.

Pricing

Many businesses adjust prices based on demand, booking time, competition, and season. The goal is to maximize revenue per customer by charging the most each is willing to pay.

Upsells

Successful businesses in this industry often have secondary sources of revenue or upsells to increase how much customers spend with them.

Examples of this include:

- **Airlines**: Baggage fees, seat selection, snacks, and in-flight internet
- **Hotels**: Breakfast, parking, spa access, early check-in, and late checkout
- **Cruises**: Shore excursions, drink packages, and casino play

These add-ons typically have very high profit margins and are critical to overall profitability.

Loyalty programs

Frequent flyer miles, hotel points, and membership tiers encourage repeat business from customers. These loyalty programs create switching costs for customers, making it more difficult for them to switch to a competitor.

Some loyalty programs are so valuable that companies sell points to partners, such as credit card companies, which creates another source of revenue for them.

Group bookings and events

Business conferences, weddings, school trips, and tours often book large blocks of rooms, flights, or tables at restaurants.

These large group events provide a significant amount of revenue from one client. Many businesses in the hospitality and travel industry have dedicated sales teams just to handle large clients.

Common industry challenges

- **High fixed costs**: Businesses in this industry typically have high fixed costs, creating pressure to keep occupancy rates high in order to be profitable

- **Seasonality**: Many businesses peak during specific months. They must generate enough revenue during their busy season to offset quieter months

- **Economic sensitivity**: In recessions, travel and leisure are among the first expenses people cut. This industry is considered a luxury for many customers

- **Labor dependence and turnover**: Success in this industry depends on frontline employees that interact with customers (e.g., housekeepers, flight attendants, chefs, tour guides). These jobs often involve long hours, modest pay, and high turnover, so staffing issues are common

- **Commoditization**: Many offerings feel similar (e.g., mid-tier hotel rooms, economy airline seats) and brand differentiation is difficult. So, businesses compete heavily on price and convenience

- **Third-party intermediaries**: Online travel agencies help drive bookings, but often charge commissions of 15-30%. Businesses in this industry need to balance reaching more customers while protecting their profit margins

Lesson #97: Transportation and Logistics Industry

The transportation and logistics industry is responsible for the movement of goods across the globe. It plays a critical role in supply chains and enabling trade.

Businesses in this industry include:

- **Freight transportation**: Trucking, rail, air freight, and maritime shipping

- **Warehousing and distribution**: Includes storage facilities and fulfillment centers that hold and manage inventory before it's shipped

- **Third-party logistics**: Companies that offer outsourced logistics services including transportation, warehousing, and inventory management

Key drivers of success

Operational efficiency

Success in the transportation and logistics industry depends on minimizing cost per mile or cost per shipment.

This includes optimizing fuel usage, reducing idle time, improving driver productivity, and minimizing empty miles when fleet return without cargo.

High utilization

There are high fixed costs in this industry because purchasing trucks, warehouses, planes, and ships is expensive. Any underutilization of fleet significantly hurts profit margins.

Coverage and scale

Companies that have a wide and flexible distribution network can offer better reach and faster service.

Additionally, the ability to scale operations quickly is critical for maintaining service levels and retaining customer contracts.

Technology and data analytics

Real-time tracking, route optimization, automated scheduling, and predictive maintenance all reduce downtime.

Advanced analytics can forecast demand, optimize fleet usage, and reduce delivery times.

Customer service and reliability

Consistent on-time delivery, clear communication, and handling of exceptions such as delays or damages are critical to customer retention.

Businesses choose logistics partners not just on price, but also on reputation and service levels.

Common industry challenges

- **High capital requirements**: Transportation and logistics is capital-intensive. Buying or leasing fleets, building warehouses, and investing in technology all require significant upfront investment

- **Fuel costs**: Fuel is one of the largest variable costs. Price spikes can quickly eliminate any profits

- **Labor shortages**: This industry often struggles to hire and retain fleet operators, such as truck drivers, due to long hours and isolation for moderate pay

- **Infrastructure limitations**: Aging roads, railways, and port infrastructure can slow delivery times and increase fleet maintenance needs

- **Last-mile delivery complexity**: Delivering packages to consumer homes is expensive and time-consuming. These deliveries are small, individual packages going to many different addresses instead of one large cargo going to one warehouse

- **Regulatory complexity**: Companies must navigate local, national, and international rules. This includes safety regulations, emission standards, driver hour limits, and customs procedures

Lesson #98: Real Estate Industry

The real estate industry revolves around buying, selling, leasing, and managing property. At its core, real estate is all about land and the things built on top of it.

Major real estate segments

There are four major segments of real estate:

1. **Residential**: Properties where people live (e.g., single-family homes, apartments, condominiums, townhouses)

2. **Commercial**: Properties used for business purposes (e.g., office buildings, retail stores, shopping centers, hotels, restaurants)

3. **Industrial**: Properties used for manufacturing, logistics, and storage (e.g., warehouses, distribution centers, factories, data centers)

4. **Land**: Undeveloped property, agricultural land, and land for future development

How real estate companies make money

There are two main ways businesses make money in real estate:

1. **Appreciation**: Property values tend to increase over time. If you sell property for a higher price than you bought it for, you'll make money

2. **Income**: Earning regular payments from rent or leases

Many real estate businesses do both.

Example: A mall operator might collect monthly rent from stores. Years later, they might decide to sell the property for a profit due to appreciation.

Key concepts in real estate

- Real estate is often bought with debt, which increases potential returns, but also increases risk

- Occupancy rate is the percentage of a building that is currently leased or rented out – higher occupancy generally means higher and more stable income

- Capitalization rate measures the return on investment for income-producing properties. It is calculated as Net Income divided by Property Value. The higher the cap rate, the higher the returns are and the faster the initial investment can be recouped

- REITs (Real Estate Investment Trusts) are companies that own real estate and pay out most of their profits as dividends to their investors

Lesson #99: Government Industry

The government industry includes all public sector agencies that provide services to citizens and operate using taxpayer funding.

Unlike companies that aim to generate profit for shareholders, government agencies exist to serve the public interest by providing essential services, maintaining infrastructure, and ensuring public safety.

How government agencies work

Government agencies operate differently from companies.

They receive funding through budget allocations rather than generating revenue through sales. Funding can come from a variety of sources, including taxes, grants, and donations.

Government agencies must spend allocated funds within the year or risk losing future funding, leading to different spending patterns than companies.

A competitive bidding process happens for most government spending on projects. These processes aim to ensure fair competition and value for taxpayers, but they can be time-consuming.

Request for Proposals (RFPs) are formal documents that outline government needs and requirements for government projects.

Contracts for government work vary significantly, from fixed-price contracts to cost-plus contracts in which the government pays for the costs plus a fee on top.

Success in government is measured by effectively delivering services within budget constraints rather than maximizing profits.

Characteristics of government agencies

- **Security clearance requirements**: Many government contracts require security clearance due to confidential information, which creates a barrier to entry for new contractors

- **Public accountability**: Extensive documentation and reporting is required, which adds administrative costs but ensures responsible use of funds

- **Political considerations**: Changes in elected leadership can dramatically change priorities, funding levels, and strategic directions

- **Extensive regulatory compliance**: Government organizations must follow strict rules, regulations, and standards that companies might not face

- **Long-term perspective**: Many public services and infrastructure projects span decades, which can conflict with short-term political cycles

Lesson #100: Non-Profit Industry

Non-profits are organizations that exist to service a mission, not to earn a profit. They focus on social, educational, environmental, or humanitarian goals.

Examples of these goals include:

- Reducing hunger and poverty

- Promoting the arts and culture

- Supporting health research

- Protecting the environment

- Advocating for social change

How non-profits operate

Unlike businesses that sell products or services for profit, non-profits get their revenue from a variety of different sources:

- Individual donations from small donors

- Grants from foundations

- Government funding through grants, contracts, and reimbursements

- Earned revenue through fees for services, product sales, or investment income

- Corporate partnerships

- Special events and fundraising activities

Non-profits are legally required to reinvest all revenue into activities that support their stated charitable or public purpose. They cannot pay profits to shareholders or owners.

However, they can pay reasonable salaries to employees and executives and keep reserves for long-term stability.

Lastly, most non-profits are tax-exempt. Non-profits do not need to pay taxes on money earned that's related to their charitable mission.

Common industry challenges

- **Funding sustainability**: Donations and grants can be unpredictable with many non-profits often relying on a few large donors

- **Resource constraints**: Budgets are tight and non-profit staff are often underpaid and overworked. Many non-profits also rely on volunteers, which can limit consistency and skill levels

- **Outcome measurement**: Unlike for-profit companies that track profit, non-profits must track impact, which is often qualitative or hard to quantify

- **Balancing mission and growth**: Growing the non-profit may risk reducing program quality

- **Stakeholder alignment**: Non-profits must balance the interests of donors, beneficiaries, board members, staff, and volunteers, all of whom may have conflicting goals or priorities

- **Regulatory burdens**: Non-profits need to follow strict rules and prove transparency and accountability, all of which can be time-consuming to document and audit

- **Public trust**: One scandal or mistake can seriously damage public credibility

14. Next Steps

Final Thoughts

Congratulations on finishing the 2-hour MBA crash course!

If you've made it to this page, you've done something that most candidates never do: develop a sharp business acumen.

You've built a foundational toolkit of 100 essential business topics and have the business intuition to think and speak like a consultant.

Think about where you started.

Maybe some of these concepts were new to you. Perhaps you had heard of certain terms but didn't really know how to apply them.

Now, you can walk into the interview room and talk about business with confidence. This is huge growth and you've earned it.

However, reading alone isn't enough. Knowledge becomes power only when it's used. So, start applying what you've learned.

Run through practice cases and put your business intuition to practice. The more you turn these business concepts into mental reflexes, the sharper you'll be in case interviews.

You've got the tools. You've built the confidence. Now, it's time to go out there and crush your case interviews.

You got this!

If there's anything I can do for you to help you land your consulting job, please let me know. I've included resources I provide to help candidates land their dream consulting job at the end of this chapter.

I'd Love to Hear From You

If you found this book helpful, I'd be incredibly grateful if you left a quick review on Amazon. It only takes about 30 seconds and it makes a huge difference in supporting me as an independent author.

Click the link below to leave a review:

https://www.amazon.com/review/create-review?asin=B0FMH4M5CS

Or simply scan this QR code with your phone:

I read every single review and yours would truly mean a lot.

Recommended Resources

Case Interviews

Case interview business knowledge is just one piece of the puzzle. To ace your case interviews and land consulting offers, you'll need to nail every single part of the case interview.

How comfortable and confident do you feel about:

- Developing structured and tailored frameworks

- Solving math problems that test your analytical thinking

- Interpreting data in the form of tables, charts, and graphs

- Answering qualitative questions that assess your business acumen and brainstorming creativity

- Proactively leading the direction of a case interview

- Delivering a clear and compelling recommendation

Learn case interviews in as little as 7 days while saving yourself 100+ hours of prep time through our comprehensive case interview course:

https://www.hackingthecaseinterview.com/courses/consulting

Some of our students have passed their first-round interviews at McKinsey, BCG, and Bain with just a week of preparation.

Consulting Behavioral and Fit Interviews

Remember that case interviews are not the only thing that show up in consulting interviews. Every consulting firm will ask you behavioral and fit interview questions.

Are you prepared to answer interview questions such as:

- Tell me about yourself

- What makes you interested in consulting?

- Why do you want to work at this firm?

- What's your greatest weakness?

- Tell me about a time when you resolved conflict in a team

- Why should we hire you?

If you want to be prepared for 98% of behavioral and fit questions in just a few hours, check out our behavioral interview course. We'll teach you exactly how to draft answers that will impress your interviewer.

https://www.hackingthecaseinterview.com/courses/consulting-behavioral-and-fit-interview-course

Consulting Resume and Cover Letter

Don't expect to get any consulting interviews if you have a poorly written resume.

Breaking into consulting is extremely competitive. You need an outstanding resume that is tailored and optimized for consulting to help you stand out from the crowd.

If you need professional help crafting the perfect consulting resume, I'd love to work with you. Transform your resume into one that will get you multiple interviews.

https://www.hackingthecaseinterview.com/courses/consulting-resume-review-and-editing

15. About the Author

Taylor Warfield

Taylor Warfield is a former Manager and interviewer at Bain & Company. He is the author of several best-selling books, including:

- Hacking the Case Interview

- The Ultimate Case Interview Workbook

- Case Interview Math, Math, Math

- Hacking the PM Interview

- How to Write a Resume That Doesn't Suck

He is the founder of HackingTheCaseInterview.com and has a YouTube channel with millions of views.

His books, online courses, and coaching have helped thousands of students and working professionals land job offers at top-tier consulting firms including McKinsey, BCG, Bain, LEK, Oliver Wyman, Strategy&, and EY-Parthenon.

www.ingramcontent.com/pod-product-compliance
Lightning Source LLC
Chambersburg PA
CBHW070646160426
43194CB00009B/1598